THE
PROPHESIED

MESSIAH

**Zola Levitt and
Thomas McCall**

PORTERFIELD PRINTING
Dallas, Texas

Dedication

The authors dedicate this book in respectful memory of Rachmiel Frydland (1919-1985). The following is a tribute written by Zola Levitt early in 1985.

I recently learned of the death of Rachmiel Frydland, the most courageous saint I ever knew. I had the honor of editing an autobiography of this one-of-a-kind Christian soldier.

It's hard to know where to begin to tell the story of a man like this one. As a Jew, he was a prodigy in the study of the Talmud and a fully qualified rabbi. As a Christian, he held degrees qualifying him as a minister and a linguist in Hebrew, Aramaic, Syriac and Arabic. In the secular world, he completed all the requirements for a Doctor's Degree at New York University but never troubled to accept the degree. The last picture I have of him was taken in an office at Jews for Jesus where he is shown stuffing envelopes.

What I remember best about this brilliant and humble servant was his amazing ministry during the Holocaust. This man smuggled himself *into* the Warsaw Ghetto in order to witness to the Jews! In a place where a veritable massacre was going on day and night, and life hung by a thread, Brother Frydland put his life on the line to testify of his Lord. I never knew a more inspiring missionary story.

During the brief period that I helped him with his writing, I was embarrassed to have to keep talking about myself. His interest in the next person was complete and sincere. He acted as if he had little to talk about and had been nowhere special. His writing was modest and simple and it was only through patient interrogation that I was able to bring out the facts of his incredible ministry.

Few outside the hard missions to the Jews know his name and he will never be regarded as an important Christian.

I know that even now he's telling the Lord that he did nothing.

There was a time in Rachmiel's life when he was entirely alone in the world. He was an Orthodox Jew who believed in Christ and he was turned away by the synagogues and finally by his church, who said that since the Nazis were in charge, Jews couldn't worship Christ in the churches! He faced nothing but enemies and the Lord put them all beneath his feet.

A great saint has gone ahead. His place will be close to the throne in the Kingdom to come.

CONTENTS

Introduction

This book was designed to amplify and clarify prophetic messages given on the television program ZOLA LEVITT PRESENTS.

When Dr. Thomas S. McCall, our biblical consultant and co-author, looked for the most dramatic and visually presentable prophecies in the Bible, he came up with the eleven we presented on the program and in this volume. It should be quickly said that there are far more prophecies than these. Some of the others we would like to have done did not have a good location site for visual purposes, or were difficult to dramatize in the medium. What we really hoped to do is just open the subject because Messianic prophecy, for all of its importance, is not very well understood today.

For the sake of our viewers, we have given a short dramatic scenario at the beginning of each chapter describing the biblical scenes which opened each program. On location we utilized Israeli actors to portray the Bible characters and more or less set the stage for the discussion on the program. These little vignettes, then, will orient the reader to the times and places of the prophecies.

There are two major kinds of biblical predictions about the Messiah. First there are direct prophecies bearing on objective events. Micah said that Messiah would be born in Bethlehem and so He was (Micah 5:2). Isaiah said He would die and be resurrected and so He was (Isa. 53). The other kind of prediction is called a "type," which is a symbol of Messiah in the Old Testament, especially those which are authorized by the New Testament. Isaac being offered in sacrifice on Mt. Moriah is a type of Messiah, as we explain. Moses, being rejected at first by his brethren and then accepted when he returns to them in a second coming, is a type of Messiah. Of course, the prophecies and types given here by no means comprise a complete list. Ingenious Bible annotators are still finding subtle references to Messiah in the Old Testament even today. The ones we have presented here are meant to be easily understood and appreciated, and perhaps to serve as examples for how we might more carefully read the statements of God's prophets.

Certain kinds of minds prefer a rational and logical approach to spiritual things, and the Bible rewards them amply. It is not necessary in true biblical faith merely to venerate the Messiah and then insist that all references point to Him. It can be proved beyond a doubt that all references point to Him. Those who, for whatever reasons, go about the hazardous task of refuting Messianic prophecies often end in terrible frustration.

A primary use of Old Testament prophecy would be in testifying to Jewish people, of course, since they hold the Old Testament to be the word of God in many cases. But it shouldn't be overlooked that any open-minded reader has to be impressed with accurate predictions of future events. Hal Lindsey's book, The Late Great Planet Earth, galvanized millions of believers and unbelievers alike a decade ago with simple comparisons of what the ancient prophets stated and how these events were working out. It is a pleasurable and profitable exercise to understand the Holy Scriptures, and particularly to appreciate their elegance and precision on the subject of Messiah.

To witness from the Old Testament was a necessary skill of the Apostles. Having only that Bible and no New Testament to refer to, they managed to ignite saving faith all over a perfectly indifferent pagan empire. Armed with the same sort of knowledge, we can possibly do the same thing again.

1

Abraham and Isaac

אברהם
יצחק

*T*he scene is ancient Mt. Moriah in the upper reaches of
the central mountain ranges at Canaan. A very aged
bearded man and a youth wearily ascend a steep and rocky
slope, carrying materials for animal sacrifice. They have a
rope, firewood, and a censor of hot coals. The old man
carries a long, sharp knife.

They pause among the windblown underbrush. Young
Isaac asks Abraham, "Father, where is the lamb?"

The old man concentrates deeply. His forehead is lined,
the sweat of a three-day journey glistening from his brow.
He speaks softly but with great force, "The Lord will
provide". Soon they arrive on the summit of the holy
mountain. Methodically and tragically Abraham binds the
one God called, "Thine only son" with the rope, and
places him on the altar of wood. He picks up the knife and
looks at it, and then raises his eyes to heaven. Isaac lies in
stunned silence watching his father looking pleadingly
into the sky. Finally, Abraham raises the knife and the boy
closes his eyes.

But all at once the raised arm is stopped and the angel of
the Lord cries out, "Lay not thine hand upon the lad," and
the shaken Abraham desists. Suddenly there is a noise and
the father and son see an unusual sight, a ram caught by
his horn in a bush.

"Behold, a ram was caught in a thicket by his horns."

"Take Thy Son"

In the long difficult relationship between God and man, that was a pristine moment. Abraham did not use his sacrificial knife on that singular day some 4,000 years ago. The Lord was testing the one He called His "friend" on that occasion. He had told Abraham to take Isaac and offer him as a "whole burnt offering", which meant slaying his son and then burning his body completely with fire. But having tested the faithful one to this extraordinary limit the Lord sent His angel to stop Abraham and provided the ram as a substitute sacrifice. Throughout the Scriptures to follow, the ram's horn, the trumpet of the Bible, will repeatedly be used when God delivers His people (as in the battle for Jericho with Joshua, Gideon's battle with the Midianites, and ultimately the rapture of the Church.)

Isaac understood the procedure of sacrifice and would have been the first to appreciate his father's unquestioning faith. Abraham had offered sacrifices on numerous occasions and Isaac had many times seen the knife, the rope, the firewood, and the hot coals. Isaac was probably a teenager by that time and he was used to his father's ways of worship. The missing element, the animal, made him inquire, but he was satisfied, as would be his descendants through the ages, with the answer "The Lord will provide".

The selection of Mt. Moriah, as it is recorded in Genesis 22, brought Abraham to what is now Jerusalem. Mt. Moriah is the name for the general range of hills or mountains surrounding the area, and also the specific name of the hill which later became the site of the Temple of God. Moriah is a sister to the upper hill of Jerusalem known as Mt. Zion. The series of remarkable spiritual events commenced by the appearance of Abraham and Isaac at Mt. Moriah continues in the same place throughout Scripture.

God chose a relatively modest land when he sent Abraham to Canaan, and out of that area He selected a rather ordinary little mountain as mountains go. He continued, however, to operate there throughout the whole of the biblical record, as we shall see.

And in the kingdom to come God will dwell among His people for a thousand years on that same mountain.

The King Priest

The mysterious Melchizekdek ("King of Righteousness") the king priest of Salem, appears during the career of Abraham. Salem was evidently one of the early names of Jerusalem and in Genesis 14 we read about its ruler. Abraham occasioned to stop at Salem returning from a conflict in which he had pursued four kings of Mesopotamia to the region of Haran, what we know as Syria today.

Somewhere above the Golan Heights he and his small band of dedicated commandos attacked the armies of the Mesopotamian kings who had previously routed Sodom and the other cities of the lower Jordan River Valley. The idea was to rescue Abraham's nephew, Lot, and certain other captives and to regain the treasures that had been taken from the Dead Sea cities. When Abraham arrived back at Salem he gave thanks to God for his victory and offered tithes through the priest of God, Melchizedek. They apparently knew each other and Melchizedek welcomed Abraham with a symbolic meal of bread and wine. The priest blessed the victorious one, and that's all that is said. Melchizedek appears and disappears in Scripture very briefly but he is considered a key personality by the writer of the book of Hebrews in the New Testament.

Melchizedek is recognized as a priest of the Most High God capable of bestowing a blessing from God on the father

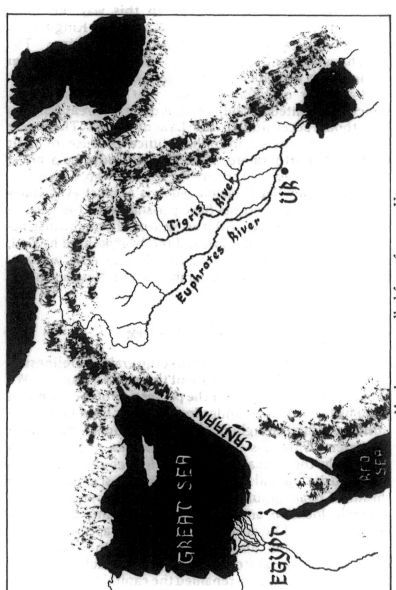

Abraham was called from far away Ur.

of the Hebrew faith, Abraham. In this way, he is an excellent type or symbol of the Messiah, our King Priest. The psalmist supplies the following information: "The Lord has sworn and will not repent, You are a priest forever according to the order of Melchizedek." (Psalm 110:4)

The writer of Hebrews notes that Melchizedek was directly appointed by God, which is quite different from the priesthood according to the Law of Moses. They were Levites and entered into their office because of their birthright. Furthermore, Melchizedek would be a priest forever, which was not true of the Levites who served only as long as they lived. Melchizedek is a priest even today while the Levitical priests have perished with the Law.

Melchizedek shares with the Messiah alone the distinction of being an eternal priest directly appointed by God, and some interpreters believe that Melchizedek was actually Christophany, an appearance of the Messiah in Old Testament times.

David The King

Centuries came and went with scriptural leisureliness as the Hebrew people thought about their holy mountain. We should appreciate that after the possession of the Promised Land by the Israelites under Joshua, they lived for several hundred years throughout the land of Canaan but not in Jerusalem. This was one of the pockets of occupation retained by the Canaanites. Now called Jebus, the city was the Jebusite capital when King David ascended to the throne of Israel around 1,000 B.C. David appreciated the strategic location and spiritual significance of the Mt. Moriah area and he devised a strategy to capture the city. After a successful campaign he renamed the place Jerusalem and declared it to be the capital of Israel (after some 3,000 years it was again renamed the capital in 1980 A.D.).

God had specified in Moses' law that He would designate a place where His name would be called and His worship established as a permanent fixture (Deut. 12). But during the time of the Judges, the Tabernacle, with its holy artifacts, was primarily located in the town of Shiloh some 15 miles north of Jerusalem. King David thought often of the God who had accompanied him into his historic duel with Goliath. II Samuel 7 records the king's great desire to build a Temple for the Lord which would at last create a permanent structure for Hebrew worship. The prophet Nathan informed David that he would not be the builder after all but that his son would build the Temple.

Satisfied with that information David went on to build the mighty kingdom of Israel in some of its most glorious days. He conducted a military census at one point to determine the strength of his army, but the Lord strongly condemned the king for this conceit. A plague was unleashed throughout Israel sending David into earnest prayer for the welfare of his people. When the angel with the plague came to the capital city he stopped dramatically on that well-remembered hill, Mt. Moriah. David immediately purchased the territory from its owner, Arunah the Jebusite, and made a sacrificial offering to the Lord at once. In this way it was determined that God had chosen the place of His worship and the site of the Temple.

The multi-talented David was deeply sincere about his relationship with God and willing to back it with his personal fortune. A gifted military commander, a statesman of great acumen and the composer of the tenderest Psalms, David combined intelligence and power in a most graceful way. He wanted to recognize God's wishes about Mt. Moriah and he organized a vast fund-raising campaign which would finally succeed in building a wonder of the world. I Chronicles 29 relates David's gathering of the leaders of the twelve tribes of Israel to inform them that he, out of his own treasury, was committing 3.6 million ounces of gold and 8.4 million ounces of silver toward the Temple project. This would amount to more than a billion dollars in today's market! It was a challenge gift meant to inspire the tribal leaders and they more than matched the king in the end. They presented 6 million ounces of gold and 12 million ounces of silver, doubling the generosity of the king.

And thus three billion of today's dollars were available for the massive project.

The First Temple

Ultimately it fell to David's equally illustrious son, Solomon to build the house of the Lord. The Beth ha Migdash, the Holy House, was the largest Temple ever constructed on earth. Considering its broad esplanades and wide spaces, porticoes and enormous walls, the massive temples of Greece and Rome would fit several times into the 34-acre Jerusalem Temple site. The Great Pyramid of Egypt would comfortably fit within its walls. It was not, of course, a single building as we think of a synagogue or a church today but rather a campus of buildings of stone construction on many levels, with ramps and pillars and avenues back and forth to accommodate virtually the entire population of the nation at one time. Mt. Moriah had indeed been honored.

The Temple functioned for nearly four centuries from 960-586 B.C. It was the place where Almighty God dwelt (Ex. 25:10) during all of the time of the Davidic monarchy from Solomon until the Babylonian captivity. The porch of the Temple was as tall as a ten story building and the sanctuary itself contained magnificent artifacts of solid gold. The inside walls were laid over with the precious cedar wood from Lebanon so that no stone showed through at any point. It was in the best estimation of the chosen people a fitting dwelling place for Almighty God Himself. Outside the sanctuary stood the bronze altar of sacrifice and the great laver holding the cleansing water for the ministrations of the priests.

The worship conducted in this marvelous atmosphere was resplendent. As the priests ministered, the Levitical choirs sang the Psalms of David and the other Psalms that we read in Scripture today. It must have been an overwhelming combination of grandeur and pandemonium when the entire male population of Israel brought sacrificial animals to the worship in that singular place.

Truth to tell, the sincerity of the worship varied over the four centuries of the Temple's existence. Sometimes there were great revivals under the kings, prophets and priests, but at other times there was laxity and even apostasy. Nevertheless, there always was a testimony for the God of Abraham, Isaac, and Jacob in the Solomonic Temple on Mt. Moriah.

Early on the Queen of Sheba had come from the far south to visit Jerusalem and its storied Temple. She concluded that all she had heard about that magnificent place was certainly true. Jerusalem must have attracted at least the amount of tourism that it does today and during the reign of Solomon, Israel dominated the Middle East.

But it all came to ashes. After Solomon, the kingdom split into North and South and the invariably hostile neighboring powers began to eye the weakened chosen people. Jerusalem was besieged and attacked on numerous occasions by the Egyptians, the Syrians, the Assryians, and even by the ten northern tribes, who had formed their own kingdom. It continued to survive under the most difficult conditions. But finally Nebuchadnezzar, the King of Babylon, succeeded in destroying the Temple and the entire city of Jerusalem in 586 B.C.

The prophet Jeremiah wept as the people of Jerusalem and Judah were taken captive to Babylon for a period of 70 years. The Temple was totally destroyed and the summit of Mt. Moriah was covered by broken stones and burned out rubble.

The Second Temple

It must have appeared to the people of Jerusalem that there was no hope. The ten northern tribes had been carried off earlier and now Judah and the capital city were vanquished. The Temple was gone and it seemed as though God Himself had turned against His chosen people. We must appreciate that Judaism at this time was 1,500 years old, a much longer span of time than that of most of the world's religions. The people could not turn away from so ancient a faith, and yet how could they go on?

The prophets who attended the captives encouraged them, however. Jeremiah's prediction that the deportation to Babylon would last 70 years was taken very seriously by the prophet Daniel, whose splendid 70 Weeks of Years prophecy reassured the captives that Jerusalem would be rebuilt and the chosen people would return to their land.

Jeremiah's prophecy about restoration was accomplished when the Persians invaded Babylon and King Cyrus decreed that the people of Jerusalem could return and rebuild their house of God.

It was a far cry from the days of wealth and military strength that accommodated the building of the first Temple. This time strong pagan neighbors objected to the idea of the Jerusalem Temple, and the Samaritans in particular constantly harassed the returning Israelites, in a situation not unlike today's. And when the foundation of the Temple was laid it seemed so pitifully small compared to the original that it was greeted with very mixed emotions:

And they sang responsively, praising and giving thanks to the Lord: "For He is good, for His mercy endures forever toward Israel." Then all the people shouted with a great shout, when they praised the Lord, because the foundation of the house of the Lord was laid.

But many of the priests and Levites and heads of the fathers' houses, who were old men, who had seen the first temple, wept with a loud voice when the foundation of this temple was laid before their eyes; yet many shouted aloud for joy."

So that the people could not discern the noise of the shout of joy from the noise of the weeping of the people, for the people shouted with a loud shout, and the sound was heard afar off.(Ezra 3:11-13)

The aged ones who had seen the first Temple and then endured all 70 years of the captivity in Babylon rejoiced and wept simultaneously. Gone was the gold and silver and beautiful woodwork that marked Solomon's overwhelming House of God and now they had to settle for what they could build with a stone in one hand and a sword in the other. However, with the urgings of the various prophets, Ezra, Zechariah and Haggai, the Temple, however modest, was completed in 516 B.C.

The second Temple was to last more than five centuries until the Romans destroyed it in 70 A.D. It began modestly but finished, under the architectural genius of King Herod, perhaps equal to or even greater than the Solomonic Temple. During the time of Jesus the paranoid Herod, who had slain members of his own family, applied his obsessive building program to Mt. Moriah. In truth he virtually rebuilt the original structure, creating a Hellen istic version of the Temple that must have amazed even the Romans.

History had again honored Mt. Moriah, which continued to be the centerpiece of the worship of God on earth. The Jewish Talmud comments on the extraordinary magnificence of the second Temple, "He who has never seen Herod's Temple has never seen a beautiful building in all his life." The prophet Haggai had spoken the truth:

> " 'The glory of this latter temple shall be
> greater than the former,' says the Lord of hosts.
> 'And in this place I will give peace,' says the
> Lord of hosts." (Haggai 2:9)

The Temple of God was again glorious, but even more so it was graced with the presence of Messiah Himself.

The biblical culmination of the lengthy and contentious history of Mt. Moriah is the sacrifice of Messiah. The holy mountain had seen every sort of triumph and disaster in the course of human affairs up to that time and it has continued in the same pattern to the present day. It remains in conflict at this writing and, according to prophecy, it will remain so until the very return of the King Himself. But that's another story.

For our purposes here, the biblical history of Mt. Moriah runs from Abraham and Isaac to Jesus Christ. The death of the Messiah crowns the mountain with an event so significant in the history of Judaism, and that of all men, that all that went before and all that followed are overshadowed.

Of course the sacrifice could not take place on the altar of the Temple itself since it had to be "outside the wall" but it was evidently still on Mt. Moriah. Two sites that have been historically claimed as the place of the death and resurrection of Christ—the Church of the Holy Sepulchre and Gordon's Calvary—are both on a continuation of the upward slope of the hill from the Temple mount north of the Temple area. Topographically they are still a part of Mt. Moriah and so Jesus was sacrificed as close as legally possible to the place where Isaac was offered in sacrifice.

The similarity of these two extraordinary events suggests a closer study of Isaac as a type of Messiah. No less a Bible teacher than the Apostle Paul thought of Abraham and Isaac as symbolic of God the Father and God the Son.

Isaac And Christ

Paul taught the Galatians a striking lesson about Abraham and Isaac in regard to the promise of Messiah (Gal. 4:22-31). He contrasted Ishmael and Isaac as being symbolic of Mt. Sinai and Jerusalem, respectively bondage and freedom. Believers in Messiah are "as Isaac was . . . children of promise".

Abraham was perceived as a type, or symbol, of God the Father, willing to offer his only son for the furtherance of the divine plan. Isaac was seen as the "only begotten son" who was willing to be sacrificed in obedience to his father, and was thus a type of Christ who loved us and gave Himself for us.

Moreover Isaac was truly the "promised seed". His birth had been promised to Abraham for some 25 years before the fulfillment came. In the same way Messiah was promised to mankind from almost the first page of the Bible. The promise began in the Garden of Eden when the Lord predicted that the seed of the woman would crush the head of the serpent (Gen. 3:15). This subtle promise was easier to appreciate with hindsight when it was repeated and

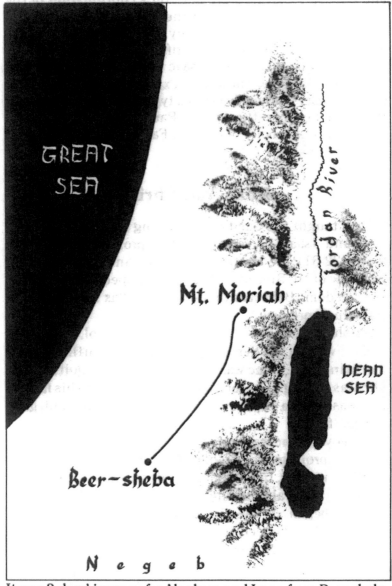

It was 3 days' journey for Abraham and Isaac from Beer-sheba to Mount Moriah.

expanded throughout the entire Old Testament. Many prophecies followed concerning the lineage of the Messiah, the manner of His birth, the city of the birth, His ministry, death and resurrection. Messiah is, in a greater way than Isaac, the Son of promise.

The birth of Isaac, like the birth of Christ, was a miracle in its own right. Isaac's mother was far too old to bear children and the Messiah was born of a virgin. God performed in both cases a divine act signalling a divine purpose.

Isaac And The Resurrection

The writer of Hebrews indicates that Isaac's survival on Mt. Moriah is a type of the resurrection of Christ. Abraham had offered Isaac, he wrote, "accounting that God was able to raise him up even from the dead from which he also received him in a figurative sense" (Heb. 11:17-19).

God had commanded Abraham to kill Isaac even while the promise was in effect that "in Isaac shall thy seed be called". Abraham might have been stymied by these apparently conflicting attitudes of God but he reasoned that if God allowed Isaac to die, He must also arrange for Isaac to be raised from the dead, according to Hebrews. Since Isaac walked away from his "death" on Mt. Moriah this act was a symbol of resurrection. Abraham had received Isaac "as a figure" of the resurrection of the dead, teaches the passage. When Jesus died on the same mountain some 2,000 years later it was a very real death, of course. However, like His ancestor Isaac, Jesus walked away from His death on Mt. Moriah. He actually arose from the dead.

Also symbolic of the resurrection is the fact that Moriah was a three-day journey from where Abraham and Isaac resided. In a similar way Messiah went on a three-day "journey" when He died and rose from the dead.

The story of Abraham and Isaac is an elegant example of the manner in which the Old Testament personalities lived out significant parts of the life of Messiah Himself. They become living predictions of how He will act and what will befall Him in His earthly ministry. In this way men could readily identify the Messiah as long as they were familiar with the scriptural types and shadows that came before. Belief in Messiah becomes more than blind faith if the Scriptures are understood. Those of Israel and the nations who came to know Him and believe in Him could do so by a kind of informed consent once they understood the beautiful symbolism of the Old Testament.

Similar stories follow, and in truth men have probably not completed the rewarding task of realizing all of the treasures so subtly woven into the Word of God.

2
Joseph
יוסף

*T*en young men are tending their flocks of sheep in the
hilly Samaritan countryside on their way to Dothan,
where they have found pasture to graze their sheep. In the
distance they see a teenage boy heading toward them,
loaded down with supplies. He is their younger brother,
Joseph. His unusual multi-colored coat can be appreciated
from quite a distance. The ten glance at each other as they
watch Joseph approach.

They have a problem with their brother. He is their
father's favorite and they are envious. They have a
problem not only with the coat but with the spiritual
provocations of Joseph. They refer to him as "the
dreamer". They talk themselves into a vengeful mood and
as Joseph reaches his brothers, they seize him and throw
him into an open pit.

Should they kill him and be rid of their troubles once
and for all? As they deliberate, a caravan of Midianites
heads toward them from the north. They are outfitted for
the long trek to Egypt. The brothers decide to avoid blood
on their hands and to sell Joseph to the traders. They will
not have to listen to any more interpretations of dreams by
the precocious Joseph and they'll make a profit as well.
Joseph is taken by the caravan and the ten sons of Jacob
dip the infuriating coat in goat's blood to show to their
father in Hebron.

Jacob is convinced of their story and overcome with
inconsolable grief, believing that his beloved son, Joseph
his favorite, has been killed by a wild beast.

The Dreamer

Joseph's ten half-brothers thought they had seen the last of him, little realizing that many years later they would meet the difficult one again in very different circumstances in Egypt. Their youngest brother, Benjamin, the other son of Jacob and Rachel, saw none of this since he was too young to tend flocks at the time. With the bloody garments as evidence, they washed their hands of the tedious favorite of the family.

Who was Joseph and why was he so despised by his brothers, the other sons of Jacob? Joseph, for one thing, was a son of Jacob's most beloved wife Rachel. Jacob, in the days of his exile from the Promised Land in Haran, fell in love with his cousin Rachel and worked seven years for her hand in marriage. Her father Laban deceived him by giving him the older daughter Leah instead, but he finally was able to marry Rachel by giving seven more years of labor. A large family ensued, with the help of the two maids of Rachel and Leah, and twelve sons and one daughter were accumulated. Joseph and Benjamin were the last two, and Rachel died in childbirth with Benjamin.

The coat was an obvious sign of favoritism given to Joseph when he became an adolescent. It is described with an unusual Hebrew word not entirely clear but translated as "a coat of many colors". It may have been actually of several different colored pieces or stripes woven together in some unique pattern. The word *"pasim"* today refers to stripes.

But it was Joseph's dreams that aggravated his brothers more than his coat. He might have employed a bit more tact but he revealed two dreams to his brothers and his parents that exacerbated the situation. One had to do with sheaves of wheat:

"Now Joseph dreamed a dream, and he told it
to his brothers; and they hated him even more.

So he said to them, 'Please hear this dream
which I have dreamed:

There we were, binding sheaves in the field.
Then behold, my sheaf arose and also stood
upright; and indeed your sheaves stood all
around and bowed down to my sheaf.'

And his brothers said to him, 'Shall you indeed
reign over us?' So they hated him even more
for his dreams and for his words." (Gen. 37:5-8)

Despite his brothers' attitude Joseph went on to reveal a
second dream that annoyed even the patient Jacob:

"Then he dreamed still another dream and told
it to his brothers, and said, 'Look, I have
dreamed another dream. And this time, the
sun, the moon, and the eleven stars bowed
down to me.'

So he told it to his father and his brothers; and
his father rebuked him and said to him, "What
is this dream that you have dreamed? Shall
your mother and I and your brothers indeed
come to bow down to the earth before you?'

And his brothers envied him, but his father
kept the matter in mind." (Gen. 37:9-11)

Thus the stage was set for the intense jealousy and
enmity of Joseph's brothers and their rejection of him at
Dothan.

Jacob and his sons lived the lives of husbandmen at
Hebron, tending their flocks and finding pasture for them
as far north as Dothan in Samaria. This Bedouin-like
existence still goes on in Israel today. They were less

nomadic than their grandfather Abraham and had more or less settled down. On the occasion related in Genesis 37, the ten sons were given the job of moving the herds along the Samaritan hills of Dothan. Joseph was sent with provisions of food. It was evidently as the brothers were taking a meal break on the difficult terrain that their envy came to a boil. The work was hard, the route was long and young Joseph had it coming, in their estimation.

Were it not for the Midianite caravan, probably headed from Gilead down to Egypt with various oriental merchandise, young Joseph might have perished altogether. Instead he would live to be the savior of his family and his dreams would be elegantly vindicated. In any case, the brothers profited with 20 pieces of silver and packed off what they considered their arrogant sibling to far-off Egypt. They must have felt guilty with the reaction of Jacob, who was completely overwhelmed by what he thought was a tragedy.

Joseph In Egypt

Joseph must have been terrified of the strange and very advanced civilization in which he found himself when the caravan arrived. He had been relegated to the position of a slave, but in the Lord's providence he was sold to an Egyptian military officer, Potiphar. That worthy held a high position as commander of the palace guard in the court of Pharaoh himself and he slowly developed considerable trust in his intelligent Hebrew slave. Joseph ultimately attained the position of overseer of Potiphar's plantation and he was a gifted and trustworthy manager. They Egyptian prospered and his appreciation of Joseph was shared by his wife.

Potiphar's duties took him away from home a good bit of the time and his wife was apparently lonely. In any case, she began a romantic campaign toward Joseph, who resisted her every advance. Totally frustrated, she claimed that Joseph was the assertive one and she accused him of rape. The diplomatic Potiphar knew Joseph better than that, however, and he intervened on Joseph's part. The hapless Hebrew slave would have been executed but as it was, he found himself in the dungeon at the imperial prison.

Joseph might have taken a dim view of life at this point; twice now, although he had done no crime, he found himself punished. He had been rejected by his brothers for a truthful reporting of his dreams and now was falsely accused and imprisoned by his Egyptian masters.

Joseph was incarcerated for at least two years but he never waivered from his faithfulness to the Lord, even under such trying circumstances. And God had not forgotten this talented one, even in a dungeon in Egypt.

At least it was a prison of good social position. Among the inmates were such distinguished unfortunates as the Pharaoh's own ex-butler and ex-baker. It seemed that they were accused of some palace intrigue and Joseph befriended them. In those two lay the first stages of Joseph's remarkable reclamation and ascendancy. In the providence of God both of the prisoners disclosed their dreams to Joseph who, of course, was able to help them with the interpretation. With his uncanny skill, Joseph accurately predicted the destiny of each of his cellmates. The butler would be restored to his favored position in the royal palace while the baker, the actual guilty party, was to be executed by Pharaoh. Joseph asked the butler to remember him once he was restored to his position. But the butler's memory proved to be a bit vague.

Two years slowly passed as events bore out that Joseph had been right in his dream interpretations. The butler was back in his enviable servant's relationship with Pharaoh and again, a dream intervened in Joseph's affairs. This time

Pharaoh himself was troubled in his sleep with a vision of plump, healthy cattle and starved, emaciated ones. The sovereign expressed his perplexity about the dream to his butler and, finally, the spared one told Pharaoh about the extraordinary Hebrew prisoner and his ability to interpret dreams.

Pharaoh ordered the prisoner brought before him and Joseph promptly gave the meaning of the dream: there would be seven years of agricultural abundance followed by seven years of drought and famine. Joseph counseled Pharaoh that he should appoint someone to prepare for this extended drought by storing up grain for a seven year period.

Deeply impressed, Pharaoh appointed none other than Joseph himself to take charge of the necessary preparations. To give Joseph the authority to levy a 20% tax on the crops in order to store grain, Pharaoh appointed him, in effect, to his cabinet. Joseph became Vice-Pharaoh of Egypt in charge of agricultural affairs, and he was as good an administrator as Pharaoh could ask for.

Joseph's dream interpretation once again proved to be absolutely correct and when famine did come to the entire Middle-Eastern area, Egypt was well prepared. The Hebrew ex-slave must have been the toast of the nation when the vast stores of grain came to good use in what would have been very hard times. The famine extended to the land of Canaan where Jacob and his eleven remaining sons had been living during all of this time. The land was parched and those who depended on herds had nowhere to turn. The large household of Jacob, which equalled the entire nation of Israel at the time (some 70 souls), were forced to resort to "foreign aid". Jacob dispatched his sons to Egypt to plead for food.

When the Hebrew strangers cautiously approached the royal palace of Egypt, they certainly didn't realize that they would be interviewed by their own brother, Joseph, whom they had sent into involuntary exile so long ago. Taken before the vice-Pharaoh they pleaded their pathetic case, not recognizing their forsaken brother who had now grown into manhood and wore the costume and spoke the language of Egypt. They asked for grain and Joseph was overcome by the situation. In one of the most emotional stories in the entire Bible, Joseph tearfully revealed himself to his brothers and they recoiled in very real fear.

Would he kill them? He certainly had every right and he was in a position of immense power. True to Joseph's dreams they were bowing to him and they could not do otherwise. But Joseph took the opportunity to teach his older brothers the ways of God. He informed them that while they had intended to do him harm the Lord had used the situation to cause good for him and for themselves under the trying circumstances. It was a grand time of repentance, confession and reconciliation. Joseph arranged for his father and the entire household to come down to Egypt and settle in the fertile land of Goshen, where they might pursue their work of shepherding and have grain enough to sustain them.

Joseph was well aware of God's plan to return the Hebrew nation to the Promised Land. He requested that they take his body back in the promised day when they left Egypt, and some four centuries later, his request was honored. In the Exodus the children of Israel carried the bones of Joseph through the wilderness and buried their provider in the land of Israel.

Joseph — Type Of Christ

Joseph's unusual life story provides a wealth of types of the Messiah. The martyred deacon, Stephen, in his remarkable and reckless speech in Jerusalem just before he

Joseph's adventuresome life reached from Dothan to the land of Goshen.

was stoned to death, taught this lesson (Acts 7:9-16). Just as Jesus is beloved and honored by God the Father, so Joseph was beloved and honored by his father, Jacob, as evidenced by the coat of many colors. The *"pasim,"* or stripes eloquently speak of the Messiah by whose stripes we are healed. And just as Joseph was considered a foolish dreamer by his brethren, Jesus is often thought of as a foolish, idealistic reformer by his brethren of Israel, and indeed, by the world. The patriarch was rejected by his brethren, sold for a few pieces of silver, and thrown into the pit. This was also fulfilled in Jesus who was rejected by His brethren of Israel, sold out by Judas for his few pieces of silver, and then thrown into the pit of crucifixion and burial. And again, just as Joseph was sent away by his brothers to the Gentiles, among whom he became a ruler, much the same happened in the case of Jesus Christ. Essentially spurned by Israel, Jesus has been, in effect, sent to the Gentiles, and He has become an ultimate spiritual ruler among them.

The lovely story of the reconciliation of Joseph and his brothers will be realized as indicated in biblical prophecy. The Bible calls the future tribulation the "time of Jacob's trouble" (Jer. 30:7). At the end of the Tribulation the Israelites who survive will be ready, willing and eager to accept Jesus as their Messiah and redeemer. When Messiah returns, He will finally be recognized by His brothers as their provider and they will "look upon him whom they have pierced" (Zech. 12:10), and ultimately be reconciled to Him in a glorious and tearful reunion among brothers.

In the typology then, Israel is in the position of the brothers of Joseph. They had two opportunities to react to the favored one of God. The first time they rejected the revelation of God in the dreams about Joseph's leadership over them, they spurned him and cast him to a foreign nation. At the second opportunity, when he displayed

himself to them in power and glory in the royal palace of
Egypt, they repented and accepted him, and his attitude
was one of brotherly reconciliation to them.

The likeness of the personalities of Jesus and Joseph is
clear; they both told their brethren straightforwardly of the
will of God and they both experienced the temporary
rejection. But the story has a happy ending and ultimately,
at the second coming, Israel will know Messiah, receive
Him and be totally reconciled to Him as He establishes His
kingdom upon the earth.

As Paul exalts:

> "For I do not desire, brethren, that you should
> be ignorant of this mystery, lest you should be
> wise in your own opinion, that hardening in
> part has happened to Israel until the fullness of
> the Gentiles has come in.
>
> And so all Israel will be saved, as it is written:
> 'The Deliverer will come out of Zion, and He
> will turn away ungodliness from Jacob;' "
> (Romans 11:25-26).

3
Moses
משה

I In the vast barren land of the Sinai desert, among
craggy mountains and rocky terrain, there stands a
large rock at the base of a hill. The aged Moses stands
before the rock agitated and angry. The children of Israel
have found themselves once again without water for their
families and livestock and they are afraid of dying of thirst.
Moses raises his well-worn shepherd's staff and smashes
two tremendous blows on the stone in front of him. At this
action, the rock splits and water in great abundance
gushes forth from within the stone and the hill beside
which it stands. Once again the Lord God of Israel has
demonstrated a miracle and cared for His chosen people in
the wilderness.

Water From The Rock

It must have been a great deal of water in order to satisfy
the thirst of the nation of Israel in the Sinai. The book of
Numbers indicates that there were some 600,000 men over
20 years of age capable of defending the nomads against
the marauding tribes of the desert. Therefore, considering
the older and younger males, women and children involved
in the Exodus and 40 years of wandering, there must have
been some 2,000,000 souls in all! Moses faced enormous
problems in leading such a vast multitude of human
beings, cattle and sheep under such miserable circumstances for so long a time. The Exodus must surely stand
alone in history, not only as an emancipation but as a

migration of an entire national group from one territory to another.

Water was everything. A day in the Sinai without it could be fatal. The remonstrations with the leader, Moses, were understandable under the circumstances and the deliverer faced increasing agitation among those he had so dramatically led across the Red Sea from bondage.

The Scriptures reveal both the nature of the miracle and the unholy frustration of Moses:

"Then the Lord spoke to Moses, saying,

Take the rod; you and your brother Aaron gather the assembly together. Speak to the rock before their eyes, and it will yield its water; thus you shall bring water for them out of the rock, and give drink to the congregation and their animals.

So Moses took the rod from before the Lord as He commanded him.

And Moses and Aaron gathered the congregation together before the rock; and he said to them, "Hear now, you rebels! Must we bring water for you out of this rock?"

Then Moses lifted his hand and struck the rock twice with his rod; and water came out abundantly, and the congregation and their animals drank.

Then the Lord spoke to Moses and Aaron, "Because you did not believe Me, to hallow Me in the eyes of the children of Israel, therefore you shall not bring this congregation into the land which I have given them." (Numbers 20:7-12)

The water came forth indeed just as God had promised. But the Lord took exception to Moses' excessive anger. The impatient one did not just speak to the rock, as the Lord ordered, but he struck it with his rod. This disobedience greatly displeased the God of Israel and so He meted out the drastic punishment of withholding the Promised Land from Moses. The lesson was about anger: God alone may be angry with the chosen people.

Moses had sinned and because of this sin he would not personally lead Israel into the Promised Land. Therefore, only two people of the generation who came out of slavery in Egypt would actually set foot in Israel: Joshua and Caleb. All of the rest of the Israelites of that generation had decided at Kadesh Barnea that it was too difficult a task to conquer the land and they too, therefore, displayed disbelief in the power of God. They would perish during the forty years in the wilderness and a new generation would go into the land. Joshua and Caleb alone had faith in God's promise and they would be fittingly rewarded later at Jericho.

On the eastern shore of the Jordan, the chosen people assembled to attack the walled city across the river and God allowed Moses a view of the Promised Land from the nearby Mt. Nebo. The venerable leader could see the Jordan valley, the Dead Sea and the hilly regions of the Promised Land. He died there on the mountain, having at least beheld his lifetime goal. And God Himself buried the fallen Moses.

His successor, Joshua, approached in prayer the formidable task of taking the land that flowed with milk and honey.

A Prophet Like Moses

As the career of Moses came to a close the Lord began revealing details about his successors. Israel was to enjoy the remarkable services of prophets and the ultimate successor

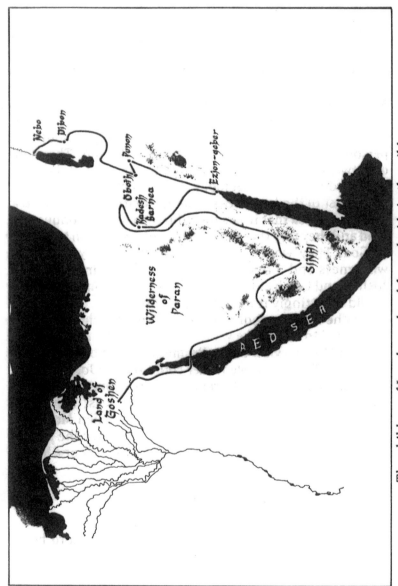

The children of Israel wandered far and wide in the wilderness.

of Moses, the Messiah. There were other patriarchs who had the gift of prophecy before Moses but he was actually the first to have what might be called the office of a prophet. There were now to be others.

Israel was to listen carefully to her prophets and to guard against false prophets who might mimic the voice of the Lord. More than this, there was to be an ultimate Prophet who had already been described as the "seed of the woman" or "Shiloh" and was now simply called "the Prophet". This greatest of future prophets is said in the record to be "like Moses":

> "The Lord your God will raise up for you a
> Prophet like me from your midst, from your
> brethren. Him you shall hear,
>
> 'I will raise up for them a Prophet like you from
> among their brethren, and will put My words in
> His mouth, and He shall speak to them all that I
> command Him.' "(Deut. 18:15, 18)

The Messiah did not come until some 14 centuries after Moses, but as we study His life and ministry we are struck by the numerous similarities of the two. Moses, like the earlier patriarchs, lived out a life of symbolism of the Messiah.

For example, both Moses and Jesus were promised deliverers of Israel. It is an important point that God revealed their coming well before they came, so that they were expected and the people could more readily obey them. Four centuries before Moses God promised Abraham that his descendants would come out of a foreign nation in which they were exiled with great power and substance:

> Then He said to Abram: "Know certainly that
> your descendants will be strangers in a land
> that is not theirs, and will serve them, and they
> will afflict them four hundred years.

"And also the nation whom they serve I will
judge; afterward they shall come out with great
possessions." (Gen. 15:13,14)

In a similar way the prophets revealed that a coming
deliverer, the Messiah, would arrive to save His people,
Israel, from bondage and oppression:

"And thus all Israel will be saved; just as it is
written, 'The Deliverer will come from Zion, He
will remove ungodliness from Jacob.' "
(Romans 11:26)

"The Redeemer will come to Zion, and to those
who turn from transgression in Jacob," says the
Lord.

"As for Me," says the Lord, "this is My covenant
with them: My Spirit who is upon you, and My
words which I have put in your mouth, shall not
depart from your mouth, nor from the mouth of
your descendants, nor from the mouth of your
descendants' descendants," says the Lord, "from
this time forevermore." (Isa. 59:20-21)

The respective rulers in the times of both Moses and Christ
reacted in the same unfortunate way to the promises of
Hebrew Scripture. The Pharaoh of Egypt implicitly believed
God's promises to Abraham, which he read with lethal
interest. He could not tolerate the idea of an increased
Hebrew population or of a deliverer of his multitude of
slaves, and he stooped to the crime of infanticide. He sought
to have all the male Hebrew infants slaughtered at birth. The
royal decree was imperfectly enforced, however, and Moses,
for one, escaped this disaster. He was rescued ironically by
Pharaoh's own daughter and raised in the pomp and
splendor of the Egyptian court. Similarly the Messiah, born

so many centuries later in Bethlehem, escaped infanticide. The mad king of that era, Herod the Great, could not tolerate the idea of another king being in the land. Therefore, believing the Hebrew Scriptures about the birth in Bethlehem, he ordered that all of the male infants in that city less than two years of age should be slaughtered. Jesus was taken away to Egypt by Joseph and Mary, and so both Moses and the Messiah experienced an early narrow escape.

In another and very striking similarity between the two personalities, both Moses and Jesus gave up a royal palace to be with the people of Israel. Moses left the sumptuous palace of Pharaoh to join his nation of common slaves (Hebrews 11:24-26). He possibly gave up the throne, since there was a tradition that this brilliant Hebrew could have been the next Pharaoh if he had pursued that course. Obviously, as a member of the court, like his ancestor Joseph, he was the possessor of great wealth and power. He gave it all up to become identified with his own Hebrew people.

Messiah did the very same thing, if we picture Him giving up the throne of heaven in order to identify Himself with Israel and the lost peoples of the world. Christ is the Creator of the universe (John 1:1). He sustains all created things by His power. And yet He was willing to leave that heavenly circumstance and descend to the earth, becoming clothed with human flesh and frailty, and to suffer the afflictions of the human race simply in order to be with His brethren.

But in these "first comings" both Moses and Jesus suffered rejection by their own people. The Hebrews knew Moses as the adopted grandson of Pharaoh, their oppressor. Now he presented himself to them as a fellow Hebrew and became involved in their disputes. While attempting to negotiate a disagreement between two Hebrew slaves he was finally asked, "Who made you a judge over us?" Moses had killed an Egyptian when he saw him beating a Hebrew slave and now the Hebrews wanted to know if he might kill them like he killed that overseer. Thus, in effect, Moses was rejected at his first coming as their deliverer. Furthermore, he was in jeopardy because of his slaying of the Egyptian official. And thus he found himself in exile among the Midianites in the Sinai desert for some 40 years. While he was there he learned the humble trade of the shepherd and took a part-Semitic, part-Gentile wife, Zipporah, a descendant of Ishmael through her father Jethro.

The echoes of the life of Messiah are compelling. At His first coming the Messiah offered Himself as the deliverer of His people Israel. While many responded positively, the leadership of the nation as a whole did not. They rejected His claims to be Messiah. And like Moses, Jesus was in jeopardy with the secular power, the Romans, as well. Like his ancestor he became, in effect, exiled among the Gentile nations for some 1,900 years. During this time Christ has taken a new people for His bride, part-Semitic and part-Gentile. His bride, the Church, is composed of believing Jews and Gentiles in this age.

The two "second comings" of these leaders are also convincingly alike. Moses returned to his people to deliver them from bondage. This time it wasn't with reasoning and judgment but with mighty miracles and the obvious power of God. As he was instructed at the remarkable scene of the burning bush, he could transform his shepherd's staff into a serpent, his hand could become leprous and then clean again, and most overwhelming of all, there would be ten devastating plagues in Egypt to confront the hard-hearted Pharaoh. With all of this miraculous evidence Israel was persuaded that Moses, at his second coming, was indeed the deliverer appointed by God to take them out of Egypt to the Promised Land.

Miracles alone were not enough but the chosen people also had to utilize the Passover lamb. As they were commanded by the Lord, they sacrificed this lamb on the night of Passover and placed the lamb's blood on the doorposts of their houses. God had said, "When I see the blood I will pass over you," and they were literally saved by the blood. Moses remained the deliverer and leader of his people through the Red Sea, the Sinai and the 40 years of wandering, to the very gates of the Promised Land.

In much the same way but on a grander scale, Christ will return to Israel with great miracles at His second coming. This time He will return not as the meek and lowly Lamb of God, but as the powerful Lion of the tribe of Judah. At His second coming Messiah will be heralded by enormous worldwide miracles, having to do with the sun, the moon, earthquakes and the war of Armageddon. Like in Egypt, all of the plagues described in the book of Revelation will terrify the enemy. At that time Christ will redeem Israel as God's Passover Lamb. The entire surviving nation of Israel will be ready to believe at this coming, as they were ready to believe Moses when he returned. When they see the miraculous powers they will receive "the One whom they pierced" (Zech. 12:10), and He will deliver them to the promised kingdom.

Moses, of course, died at Nebo and was not able personally to bring the chosen people into the land. That task fell to his successor, Joshua, but the symbolism continues. Joshua is also a persuasive type of Christ. His very name is the same, the equivalent of *Yeshua*, Jesus' name in Hebrew. Joshua, the leader of Israel, delivered his people into the Promised Land at Jericho with shouts and with trumpets, the ram's horns. We have seen previously how Isaac, the father of all of Israel, was delivered by the ram's horn on Mt. Moriah, when the animal was caught in the thicket. Messiah will also deliver His people with the sounds of shouts and trumpets when He initiates the victory of His second coming:

> For the Lord Himself will descend from heaven
> with a shout, with the voice of an archangel,
> and with the trumpet of God. And the dead in
> Christ will rise first.
>
> Then we who are alive and remain shall be
> caught up together with them in the clouds to
> meet the Lord in the air. And thus we shall
> always be with the Lord. (I Thess. 4:16-17)

Like His namesake Joshua at Jericho then, *Yeshua* will deliver His chosen people to their promised kingdom with the sound of the shouts and the trumpets.

The victory of the chosen people in the Promised Land was initiated at Jericho and so the Messiah will initiate the great events of His second coming at the Rapture of the Church. The chosen people continued on to occupy their kingdom. Similarly, the Rapture will be the first stage of the great victory of the saints who will go on to occupy their kingdom ("the meek shall inherit the earth"). Messiah will rule for 1,000 years in the Promised Land. *

In a stunning way, then, the entire series of events of the Exodus predict the plan of salvation of the New Testament. From the bitter herbs and blood of the lamb in Egypt to the triumphant shouts and trumpets of Jericho, the chosen people experienced a delivery from bondage into the Promised Land. In like manner, the Church, and each member of the Church, proceeds from the bitter herbs of slavery to sin through the blood of the Lamb and finally the shouts and the trumpets that herald the occupation of the promised kingdom to come.

---

* *For further information on this subject, see the authors' book* Raptured, *Harvest House, 1975.*

4
David
דוד

A *teenage boy is sitting beside a tree surrounded by a herd of sheep calmly grazing in a verdant pasture. The sleepy village of Bethlehem can be seen in the distance. Young David holds in his hands a musical instrument, a lyre, which he strums while he sings to his sheep and for his own diversion. Soon the prophet Samuel will come with a fateful duty to perform for the Lord. The youngster will be anointed to be the next king of Israel. He will yet face the mighty Goliath and will go on to live one of the most fascinating lifetimes to be found in the Scriptures or anywhere else. One can hear in the background the magnificent lyrics of the 23rd Psalm, one of the mightiest of his mighty works.*

Shepherd, Soldier, King

David in his youth was a singularly sensitive and thoughtful shepherd. He believed deeply in the God of Israel and he sang sweet songs to that effect. He was to grow into what God called "a man after my own heart."

In ancient Israel, being anointed by a prophet to become king and actually ascending to the throne were quite different things. It remained for the Lord to work out the details and justify the anointing. David was to become a national hero when he met Goliath on the field of battle, and then an outlaw when the maddened King Saul tried to destroy his former champion. The high drama that always

47

followed the life of David accompanied him to the throne, where his passion for Bathsheba led him into serious sin. He suffered piteously over the death of two sons, one at birth and the other, Absalom, in open rebellion against the throne. His son, Solomon, by Bathsheba, was to become the next king but not until much devastating palace intrigue and political assassinations had grieved Israel.

David was inconsolably stricken over Absalom's death and wept, "Absalom, O my son Absalom, would God I had died for you." The massive tomb in the Kidron valley at the foot of the Temple mount called the Tomb of Absalom is the traditional site of the burial of this favored son.

Genealogy Of David

When Samuel approached the house of Jesse, David's father, to anoint the next king, readers of Scripture would not have been completely surprised. Jesse and his sons were of the tribe of Judah and the prophecy of their ancestor Jacob had established this tribe as the royal line of Israel:

> "The scepter shall not depart from Judah, nor a
> lawgiver from between his feet, until Shiloh
> comes; and to Him shall be the obedience of
> the people." (Gen. 49:10)

Jacob had twelve sons, of course, but the Lord led him to make this significant statement of destiny about Judah, who was otherwise undistinguished. The kings of Israel would come out of this tribe, including the ultimate king, the Messiah, who is here designated as Shiloh, a derivative of the Hebrew root for "peace".

One would expect, then, that from this point on, the primary leadership of Israel would be of Judah. However, from the time of Judah until David the shepherd boy,

nearly 800 years, scarcely any leader of national promi-
nence comes from the tribe of Judah. Moses came out of
the tribe of Levi and his successor, Joshua, was from
Ephraim. Throughout the 400 year history of the Judges in
the Promised Land, none of those leaders are indicated as
having come from Judah. Finally, after the Judges, when
the nation asked the Lord to appoint a king over them, Saul
of the tribe of Benjamin was selected. Contrary to the
prophecy, it seemed as though the tribe of Judah was
purposely omitted as a source for national leadership
throughout all of those generations while all the other
tribes were so honored.

But when Saul was found in disfavor with the Lord and
with his prophet, Samuel, God suddenly chose a teenage
shepherd boy in Bethlehem. At last the tribe of Judah is
selected, but why so late?

The delay may be the result of an early law God made
concerning illegitimate births in the congregation of
Israel. If we look back through the genealogy of David in
Ruth 4:18-22, we find that it begins with his ancestor
Perez. Perez is known for nothing else but being the
beginning of this particular genealogy and that is most
curious. Why did David's genealogy not begin with father
Abraham or Judah himself?

Looking into the background of Perez we may be able to
uncover the problem. He was born to Judah and Tamar but
those two were not husband and wife. In the remarkable
chapter Genesis 38, the story is revealed of Tamar, who was
the childless daughter-in-law of Judah. She had been
widowed and her husband's brother had refused to have
children with her as was the tradition of the times.
Therefore, she had no sons and the royal line would have
stopped. To solve her problem, she posed as a prostitute
and entrapped the indiscreet Judah. Tamar bore twin sons
including Perez, and thus the tribe of Judah continued.

But now it was in violation of the law given later in Deuteronomy 23:2, which states that the descendants of an illegitimate one could not "enter into the congregation of the Lord" for ten generations. The law was evidently made to serve as a deterrence to adultery but the Lord Himself apparently kept it to the letter. There were exactly ten generations from Perez to David and in all that time, scarcely any son of Judah ever led Israel despite the prophecy by Jacob.

In a way then, God is a good example to His chosen people. It was a hard law but the Almighty appears to have delayed the fulfillment of His own prophecy in order to see that it was kept.

David And The Temple

David at first ruled Israel from Hebron while Jerusalem was in Jebusite hands. But he always coveted the strategically located capital for good military and spiritual reasons, as we have seen. His idea of building a permanent structure for the worship of the Lord on Mt. Moriah is recorded in II Samuel 7:1-17.

When David consulted with his court prophet, Nathan, about the Temple project, the Lord's spokesman was elated and gave his unqualified support. But later God revealed to Nathan that while the Lord was greatly pleased with the idea of moving His earthly residence from the tent of the Tabernacle to the permanent structure of a splendid stone Temple, David would not construct it. Solomon, the king of peace, was to be the Temple builder but the Almighty had a consolation prize of tremendous significance for David.

God so appreciated David's desire to build God's house that He stated through the prophet that God would build

David's house. And moreover, He would see that the line of David would become an eternal dynasty. The Davidic Covenant promises that out of respect for David's concern to build the Temple, David would have a great name historically, Israel would have permanent national continuity, David's successor would actually build the Temple, and David's dynasty would endure forever.

All of these things came to pass, and most particularly, the promise of the eternal dynasty. It is realized in David's great son, the Messiah, the descendant of David who will reign for all eternity. The Messiah was the direct descendant of King David and will continue His royal reign forever.

David's Lord

David was not only a great soldier, statesman, and musician, but in a very real way, he was also a prophet. He was the author of most of the Psalms, which Jesus loved and quoted often.

During the week before His crucifixion Jesus confronted the Pharisees with a penetrating question about the Messiah from the Psalms:

"While the Pharisees were gathered together, Jesus asked them,

saying, 'What do you think about the Christ? Whose Son is He?' They said to Him, 'The Son of David.'

He said to them, 'How then does David in the Spirit call Him 'Lord,' saying:

'The Lord said to my Lord, 'Sit at My right hand, till I make Your enemies Your footstool'?

'If David then calls Him 'Lord,' how is He his Son?'

And no one was able to answer Him a word, nor
from that day on did anyone dare question Him
anymore."
(Matthew 22:41-46)

The Pharisees were given to trying to trip up Jesus on
scriptural grounds, but they had a hopeless task. On this
occasion He asked them whose son the Messiah was
supposed to be. It was certainly common knowledge
among the Jewish people that Messiah was to be a
descendant of David and He is frequently referred to in
their literature as "the Son of David" (as He is in the
opening verse of the New Testament). The Pharisees
answered the easy question quickly. But then Jesus
inquired as to why David addressed the Messiah as his
"Lord" if he is merely his son, or descendant. Jesus quoted
from Psalm 110 in the passage above and the implication
is, of course, that a father does not ordinarily address his
son as "Lord". This remarkable son of David must be more
than a mere descendant; He must also be the Son of God.
So it was that God the Father said to God the Messiah, "Sit
at my right hand". If the Messiah is David's Lord, argued
Jesus, then the Messiah is God. Thus David's son is also
God's Son.

It was impossible for the best scriptural analysts of Israel
to confront the Messiah with Scripture. He was biblically
adept. Matthew 23 states that after this skillful exegesis by
our Lord, no one dared ask Him any more questions.

David And The Resurrection

King David not only prophesied the deity of the Messiah
but also His resurrection from the dead. Several passages
in the Old Testament indicate the death of Messiah, such as
Isaiah 53 and Psalm 22, but many Bible students are not

aware of the primary Old Testament prophecy about Messiah's resurrection. This is found in David's Psalm 16:

"I have set the Lord always before me; Because
He is at my right hand I shall not be moved.

Therefore my heart is glad, and my glory
rejoices; My flesh also will rest in hope.

For you will not leave my soul in Sheol, Nor
will You allow Your Holy One to see
corruption." (Psalm 16:8-10)

The statement "nor will you allow your Holy One to see corruption," was crucial to the apostles of the New Testament church. Both Peter on the day of Pentecost, and Paul in the synagogue at Antioch, utilized this passage to prove that the Messiah had to rise from the dead.

At Pentecost Peter explained that David was not speaking of himself as the "Holy One" because, as his audience well knew, David was buried in a well-known marked tomb there in Jerusalem. Evidently the Jewish people of that day paid their respects to the fallen sovereign just as they do in the present generation. David's body had long ago decayed in the grave but David foresaw that his son, his great descendant, the Messiah, would not decay in the grave. He would die indeed but His body would not remain in the grave. Peter's argument went:

"Men and brethren, let me speak freely to you
of the patriarch David, that he is both dead and
buried, and his tomb is with us to this day.

"Therefore, being a prophet, and knowing that
God had sworn with an oath to him that of the
fruit of his body, according to the flesh, He
would raise up the Christ to set on his throne,

> "he, foreseeing this, spoke concerning the
> resurrection of the Christ, that His soul was
> not left in Hades, nor did His flesh see
> corruption.
>
> "This Jesus God has raised up, of which we are
> all witnesses." (Acts 2:29-32)

The facts of the prophecy are these: the Holy One is seen as being dead, His body is in the grave, His soul is in Sheol. But His soul would not remain in Sheol and His body would not decay. Instead, God would show Him "the path of life," or raise Him from the dead (Psalm 16:11). As Peter and Paul independently interpreted it, this meant that Messiah would have to be raised from the dead before physical decay set in on His body, which would have been in about 3 days. Thus the Messiah had to rise from the dead within a 3 day period, and this Jesus Himself prophesied.

The argument had great force at Pentecost because it was only 50 days after the resurrection and the population of Israel and their Roman occupational government were confronted with the empty tomb of the Messiah. Peter's explanation came at a critical time.

David's Psalm 16, then, contains essentially the only passage in the Old Testament with a specific prophecy about the resurrection of the Messiah, although it is intimated in Isaiah 53 and in the type of Jonah and the fish (3 days and 3 nights).

In the perspective of the times we should realize that not everyone was a Bible reader and the stories of Messiah had become legendary. To some He would be a great general and to others a king. It was not said so much that He actually would be God. But generals and kings do not rise from the dead and with hindsight, and equipped with David's prophecy, those of the times could fully appreciate the true nature and position of David's greatest descendant.

5

Solomon

שלמה

*K*ing Solomon is seen in splendid royal attire. He is youthful and imperially handsome. He is looking at work being done by two stone masons on a large stone being prepared for use in the Temple structure. He holds in his hands the equivalent of blueprints for the construction of the Temple of God. A narrator relates the information given in I Kings 6:1-2, 11-14, concerning the construction of the most magnificent Temple ever made by human hands.

The Temple Builder

King Solomon is remembered as the builder of the mighty first Temple of the Lord in Jerusalem. We have already seen how the Temple was renowned in its contemporary world and it has not lost its luster in historical memory. But it is difficult to find any archeological remains of the Solomonic Temple. Destruction and rebuilding has taken place many times over on Mt. Moriah and the original construction materials lie buried below the present structures. Sometimes stones were re-used in later periods since stones are hard to move from place to place, but Solomon's materials, being the first on the site, would be on the lowest level.

It should be understood that the Western Wall, like the other walls that surround the Temple mount, is a retaining wall that supported the broad esplanade that covers the summit of Mt. Moriah. Only about the top half of the Western Wall is exposed above the surface of the ground today. The remaining part of the wall still lies below ground level, down to where the street went through the Tyropean valley at the base of Mt. Moriah during biblical times. The stones in the Western Wall go back as far as the time of the second Temple (516 B.C. — 70 A.D.), but most are from the Moslem era (650 — 1917 A.D.)

Modern archeologists, however, have dug beneath the surface level at certain points toward the ancient street level and in the process they have uncovered some of Solomon's stones. Near the bottom of the wall lie very large, well-machined stones laid by Solomon around 960 B.C. In few other lands can men today find any artifact approaching 3,000 years old. In Israel alone do such ancient relics represent exactly the same culture, religion, language, and so forth. An inscription found along the southern end of the Western Wall was carved in Hebrew some 17 centuries ago but can still be readily understood by the modern populace. It praises the glory of the city of God.

We have already spoken of the fact that Solomon achieved a wonder of the ancient world. The Temples of Egypt, Assyria and Greece are comparable but not in magnitude. The Queen of Sheba's arduous journey to see the Solomonic Temple was more than justified. She was so impressed by what she saw, and by the wisdom of Solomon, that she acknowledged that "the half had not been told" to her.

Not only was the structure of the Temple beautiful to look at but it must have been wonderful to observe the worship as well. The almost symphonic music of the Levitical priests and the antiphonal singing of the songs must have been glorious indeed. And the very activity of

THE KINGDOM OF DAVID AND SOLOMON

Euphrates

Tiphsah

Hamath

Arvad

Tadmor

Lebo-hamath

Gebal

GREAT SEA

Damascus

Tyre

Rabbath-bene-ammon

Jerusalem

Karkor

Gaza

Elath

RED SEA

RIVER NILE

In its golden age Israel controlled vast territories.

the place, the sacrifices, the enormous multitudes of
people and the knowledge that Almighty God Himself
dwelt in the inner chamber of the sanctuary building — the
Holy of Holies — made Mt. Moriah a one-of-a-kind
religious experience.

It is sometimes suggested in Christian writing that the
Temple was not so valued by the Lord and that He favored
Moses' Tabernacle in the desert. The Tabernacle was
simpler and showed more humility, goes this reasoning. It
was built to precise specifications given by God Himself in
Exodus 25-30. But according to the scriptural record, the
Lord was completely satisfied with the Temple:

> "Now when Solomon had finished praying, fire
> came down from heaven and consumed the
> burnt offering and the sacrifices; and the glory
> of the Lord filled the temple.
>
> And the priests could not enter the house of
> the Lord, because the glory of the Lord has
> filled the Lord's house.
>
> When all the children of Israel saw how the
> fire came down, and the glory of the Lord on
> the temple, they bowed their faces to the
> ground on the pavement, and worshiped and
> praised the Lord, saying: 'For He is good, for
> His mercy endures forever.'"
> (II Chronicles 7:1-3)

God demonstrated His full acceptance of Solomon's
Temple by filling it with the cloud of the Shekinah glory at
the time of the dedication. The glory of the Lord shown
forth from the Holy of Holies and was so overwhelming
that the priests could not officiate in the building for some
time. It would be hard to conclude in the face of such
miracles that Jehovah was not pleased with the new House
of God.

Solomon gets the credit biblically for the construction of the Temple but we have already reviewed that it was originally his father David's idea. In any case, David must have been gratified from heaven that the Ark of the Covenant was at last transferred from the nomadic Tabernacle tent to the more permanent structure of the Temple on Mt. Moriah. We saw that at today's prices, the cost of the Temple in just the gold and silver utilized was over 3 billion dollars and we can be assured that it was one of the most God-glorifying projects Jerusalem has ever seen. The magnificent Jerusalem House of God was a shining testimony to the Lord in the midst of a largely pagan, idol-worshipping part of the world.

Solomon, King Of Peace

Solomon's name means "peace" and Israel was indeed at peace in his time. In contrast to most of the monarchs of antiquity, who of necessity had to be field marshals of their armies as well, Solomon, in his wisdom, maintained a completely peaceful administration. From the almost steady military contests of the reign of King Saul through the relatively more stable later years of David, Israel had gathered territory and subdued its enemies. Now under Solomon, an expert conductor of foreign affairs, Israel's boundaries were consolidated and then extended to its greatest dominion of history.

The reign of Solomon was Israel's golden age. Just as the empires of Egypt, Greece and Rome had their great days when they flourished with architecture, engineering, philosophy and literature, so Israel had its period of enlightenment and power in the midst of the 10th century B.C. And it bears stating that Israel's golden age was filled with faith and was uniquely spiritual. It was characterized by the Torah, the Law of God, and the worship of Jehovah in

The Ark of the Covenant at last was carried into Jerusalem.

His Temple. No other kingdom had such admirable and distinctive social and moral values as did Israel, able at last to utilize fully the gift of the Old Testament law.

It was a relatively quiescent period in general in the area, unlike in the times of Christ or in modern times. Both Egypt and Mesopotamia, the great powers to the south and north respectively, conducted reasonable, mutually profitable relations with the government of Solomon and acknowledged Israel's position among nations. Solomon's mercantile fleets and mining expeditions into far-off lands spread the influence of the chosen people throughout the known world.

Some have suggested that Solomon, through his combination of diplomacy, military presence and trade fulfilled the entire land grant that was given by God to Abraham. It is interesting to compare the original land grant, still in force today of course, with the hegemony of Israel under King Solomon:

> "On the same day the Lord made a covenant
> with Abram, saying: 'To your descendants I
> have given this land, from the river of Egypt to
> the great river, the River Euphrates."
> (Genesis 15:18)

> "So Solomon reigned over all kingdoms from
> the River to the land of the Philistines, as far
> as the border of Egypt. They brought tribute
> and served Solomon all the days of his life."
> (I Kings 4:21)

Most interpreters believe that the "river of Egypt" is not the Nile but the itinerant stream in the Sinai Desert that flows into the Mediterranean called the Wadi el Arish. This smaller body of water is sometimes called the river of Egypt and it is generally believed that it is the boundary referred to in I Kings 4:21 and 8:65. But others hold that the river of

Egypt in the divine land grant is actually the Nile. King
Solomon's holdings did not extend to the Nile, and
therefore, if that is the river that is meant, Solomon's
boundaries were not the fulfillment of the Abrahamic
Covenant.

On the Euphrates side, while the Israelites did not
actually occupy the territory beyond the Golan Heights
through Damascus and on to the river, this area was
subjugated to Solomon and paid tributory taxes to him. The
Abrahamic land grant seems to speak of a full occupation of
the territory, however, and its fulfillment probably awaits the
second coming of Messiah and the establishment of His
millenial kingdom. Solomon's reign may be regarded as
something of a foretaste of what the future golden age of
Israel will be.

(The other boundaries of the land grant were the
Mediterranean Sea on the west and perhaps the Jordan River
and its valley extending from the Arabah Rift on the south up
through Galilee and then north. However, some of the Israeli
tribes eventually settled on the east side of the Jordan in
Bashan and Gilead. That would make the eastern boundary
of the land grant the plateau area to the east of the Jordan
River Valley. The imprecise terms of the grant may indicate
that we need the second coming of the Messiah to fill in all
the details).

The Messiah, of whom Solomon is a symbol in terms of his
kingly prerogatives, will establish the territory of Israel at its
fullest extent and will reign not only over Israel but the
entire world. As the prophet Isaiah puts it, "of the increase of
His government there shall be no end." (Isaiah 9:7)

Solomon And His Bride

King Solomon is seen as a bridegroom in the elegant but
difficult to interpret Song of Solomon. The book makes
lovely reading because it describes the idyllic romance

between young King Solomon and his beloved bride from the Sharon Valley. But the story is difficult to interpret because, like a love relationship itself, it hesitates and restarts and it contains memories and flashbacks. The chronology and even the personalities involved are not entirely clear throughout the book. Though written some 3,000 years ago, it resembles a kind of "stream of consciousness" love story that we might see in a modern novel or movie.

What is clear, with the help of the New Testament pictures of Messiah as the bridegroom and the Church as His bride, is that this is a love story. And the love story concerns a king and his much less royal bride.

Throughout the romantic little book the lovers give poetic descriptions of each other. The king goes out into the countryside disguised and is met by the young woman of the fields. She describes him as the Rose of Sharon and compares him to the bright morning star. She is apparently a peasant girl whose family has a farm in the Sharon Valley, which is a sloping, fertile agricultural area between Samaria and the Mediterranean Sea. The king describes her as a most comely maiden although the narrative tells us that her skin has been sunburned by the long hours she has spent in the fields.

The young couple enjoy a wonderful courtship, marriage and honeymoon, although their relationship is clouded by some disruptions and difficult worldly circumstances. Flashbacks to other times and places color in the some- times confusing but all too realistic details of a relation- ship of love.

The love relationship of man and woman is a major theme of the Scriptures from the Garden of Eden to the end of the Bible, when the marriage of the Lamb will come (Rev. 19:7,8). Jehovah is seen as the husband of Israel in the book of Hosea, and Christ is seen as the bridegroom of the Church in the New Testament:

> "Husbands, love your wives, just as Christ also
> loved the church and gave Himself for it,
>
> that He might sanctify and cleanse it with the
> washing of water by the word,
>
> that He might present it to Himself a glorious
> church, not having spot or wrinkle or any such
> thing, but that it should be holy and without
> blemish." (Eph. 5:25-27)

With these comparisons in mind, the Song of Solomon
emerges as a lovely illustration of how Christ the King
descended disguised from heaven in order to woo His bride,
the Church, and purchase her. We are the earthly bride,
sunburned with the workaday world of human life and
tainted with the sin nature. Nevertheless, the King has
loved us and given Himself for us. We the Bride enjoy a love
relationship with this King now, and in the ultimate
consummation we shall be His wife. However, we live in a
very real world and, just as in the case of Solomon and his
bride, there are many difficulties in our relationship with
the Lord and disruptions of our fellowship because of
worldly circumstances.

Solomon, then, drawn as he is in the Song of Solomon,
is a symbol of the greater King, the Messiah, in His role of
lover, bridegroom, and husband.

Solomon And Wisdom

Both Solomon and Jesus were characterized by their
uncanny wisdom. King Solomon was a most gifted and
accomplished ruler in terms of his mental abilities. He
handed down to us some of the most subtle and majestic
writings of the Old Testament. He was an administrator of
consummate skill and he was talented as a composer, poet

and scientist. He produced 3,000 proverbs, many being inspired of God and incorporated into the book of Proverbs. He enjoyed a reputation for brilliance from Egypt to Mesopotamia.

In the case of Jesus Christ, Scripture tells us that in Him dwelt all of the wisdom of the Eternal God. His teachings and His sayings ring with divine wisdom.

The wisdom of Solomon was evidenced early in his reign and he impressed his subjects in his youth with the difficult decision of the two harlots. The story is familiar to most readers of the Bible. Two prostitutes lived together and they had children in the same week. During the night one of the young mothers accidentally smothered her baby and swapped infants with the other one. She then claimed that the living baby was hers. The lower courts were unable to reach a fair decision in this highly charged case. It was appealed up through the judicial system of Jerusalem without satisfactory conclusion until it was brought before the King. Young Solomon heard the testimony and then sent for a sword. He announced that he would cut the baby in half and give 50% to each woman. This shocking proposition had distinctly different effects on the two women. The true mother begged King Solomon to spare the child while the other could feign no more than wounded indifference. Thus the youthful king put the child with the right mother and the people of Israel were highly impressed with Solomon's understanding and intelligence.

Solomon's wisdom, like Christ's, was more than just human but really divine. When he ascended to the throne the king asked God for wisdom more than anything else. Jehovah was pleased to give Solomon much more than he asked for:

"Therefore give to Your servant an
understanding heart to judge Your people, that I

may discern between good and evil. For who is
able to judge this great people of Yours?"

And the speech pleased the Lord, that Solomon
had asked this thing.

Then God said to him: 'Because you have asked
this thing, and have not asked long life for
yourself, nor have asked riches for yourself, nor
have asked the life of your enemies, but have
asked for yourself understanding to discern
justice,

behold, I have done according to your words;
see, I have given you a wise and understanding
heart, so that there has not been anyone like
you before you, nor shall any like you arise
after you.

And I have also given you what you have not
asked: both riches and honor, so that there
shall not be anyone like you among the kings
all your days.' " (I Kings 3:9-13)

Solomon shows a Christ-like humility in his prayer, not
asking for the wealth and power that ordinary men might
value. In His response, the Lord confirmed to Solomon
that he would be the wisest of kings and that in addition He
would give to Solomon what he did not ask for, which was
wealth, power, and possessions beyond that of any king of
his time. And Solomon did gather all those things in good
measure.

Where wisdom is concerned the gospel certifies that "a
greater than Solomon" has been in our midst. While
Solomon is a type of Messiah in his wisdom, Christ is much
more than a wise person:

"For in Him dwells all the fullness of the
Godhead bodily." (Colossians 2:9)

Like Almighty God Himself, the Messiah is omniscient. He knows all and has revealed God's wisdom to us. The wisdom of God is not equivalent to the wisdom of men, however. It is very different. The wisdom of the cross is said in Scripture to be "foolishness" to mankind (I Cor. 1:23). The wisdom of the cross is that the human race has sinned and is separated from the Creator. The death of the Son of God was needed upon the cross as a reconciliation between man and God. By receiving this sacrifice, by believing in it and living by it, we have the forgiveness of sin and reconciliation with God. All of this makes good sense to the believer, who has also been given the wisdom of God. But to the unbelieving world that simple philosophy is unmitigated foolishness and makes no sense at all.

The New Testament gives a compelling example of how the wisdom of the resurrection is foolishness to human philosophers. Paul speaks to the Greek philosophers in Athens about Jesus and the resurrection from the dead, and he receives a certain amount of derision, though some in that crowd said they would like to hear more. Messiah's resurrection is no less than a guarantee of eternal life for each believer but it falls on deaf ears to those who do not believe.

How great is the wisdom of God that was manifested through Solomon millenia ago, and has now been revealed through Messiah in this age.

Types Of Messiah

King Solomon then, like the other personalities we have looked at above, lived out a life of symbolism of Messiah if we look carefully at the details. Like Christ, he is the great Temple-builder. Messiah will construct the ultimate House of

God on Mt. Moriah and reign in the 1,000 year kingdom to come. This Millenial Temple will be the most splendid ever seen on earth, as was Solomon's in its time.

Solomon's magnificent Temple truly improved upon the Tabernacle, as the salvation in Christ improved upon the delivery out of Egypt and the law in the wilderness. Grace provides a greater reconciliation to God than law.

King Solomon was admired by the Gentiles of the kingdoms outside Israel and one of them, the Queen of Sheba, actually came in person to admire him.

Solomon realized his father's greatest ambition when he accomplished the building of the House of God and Jesus has accomplished His father's "dream" in reconciling men to God by His sacrifice.

Solomon was the king of peace and Jesus is the Prince of Peace. Both enjoy reigns marked by a time of peace on earth.

Solomon possessed immense power and a kingdom of great magnitude. Christ in His return will alone rule the entire world and all nations will bow before Him. (Zech. 14:16)

Just as Solomon was the bridegroom in the Song of Solomon so the Lord Jesus is the bridegroom and will be the husband in the kingdom to come.

And finally, that uncanny divine wisdom that emanated from King Solomon was seen once again in history when a virtually uneducated carpenter's son from Nazareth taught and fulfilled the word of God.

6

Jonah
יונה

*O*n a deserted beach along the Mediterranean coast-
line of Israel a huge fish glides very close to the sand.
*Out of the shallows a human form emerges, staggering
painfully toward the shore. He struggles on to the beach,
terrible in appearance, disfigured and covered with green
slime and seaweed. He collapses in exhaustion on the
sand. The narrator explains that this is God's reluctant and
now repentant missionary, Jonah. He has a job to do at the
dreaded capital of the Assyrians, Nineveh, and he is now
ready to do it.*

The Unwilling Servant

Jonah may be the most reluctant servant of God in the
whole Bible. He did not want to do as the Lord commanded
him and he had his reasons.

Sometime around 760 B.C. the Lord commissioned
Jonah for the strange task of going to Nineveh, the capital
of Assyria. His duty was to warn that great city that it would
be destroyed in 40 days if the people did not repent of their
sins. The God of Israel was out of patience with that pagan
society.

Certain biblical personalities were *hesitant* about God's
instructions, such as Moses or Gideon, but Jonah absolutely *fled* the will of the Lord. Instead of heading east from
Israel to Assyria, he ran in the opposite direction, westward, intending to sail to Tarshish from the harbor of
Joppa, or modern Jaffa. Many interpreters believe that

Tarshish is the ancient name of Spain, on the far western shore of the Mediterranean. But in any case, Jonah meant to head the other way.

Why did the prophet so flagrantly disobey the Lord? A clue lies in Jonah's attitude toward the salvation of Nineveh, which actually did come to pass. Toward the end of this brief and unique book the prophet remonstrates with his God about the success of his mission:

> "But it displeased Jonah exceedingly, and he became angry.
>
> So he prayed to the Lord, and said, 'Ah, Lord, was not this what I said when I was still in my country? Therefore I fled previously to Tarshish; for I know that You are a gracious and merciful God, slow to anger and abundant in loving-kindness, One who relents from doing harm.' "
> (Jonah 4:1-2)

Jonah seems calloused but we must appreciate that he grew up in a time of dread fear of powerful Assyria. It was one of the most voracious pagan military empires of all time, known far and wide for its cruelty toward its vanquished enemies. The Assyrians casually displaced whole cultures, taking the people where it would do them the most economic good and replacing nations with nations as one might move cattle from pasture to pasture. The culture and historical identity of advanced civilizations was thus disrupted. And Assyria was pagan in the extreme. In Nineveh a vast pantheon of idolatrous gods were worshipped, including Dagon, the fish-god, who was also worshipped by the Canaanites and throughout the ancient world.

Furthermore, the Israeli prophets of the Lord had already designated Assyria as an ultimate enemy of Israel. Hosea, a contemporary of Jonah, predicted that Israel, the northern

Hebrew kingdom, would be devoured by the pagan conquerors:

> "Israel is swallowed up; now they are among the
> Gentiles like a vessel in which there is no
> pleasure. For they have gone up to Assyria, like
> a wild donkey alone by itself; Ephraim has hired
> lovers." (Hosea 8:8,9; see also 8:1)

Thus Jonah, certainly a God-fearing man, had good scriptural reason to view Assyria as a mortal threat. And he was astonished with God's command that he should warn them of the coming destruction. We can well imagine his dilemma. For him to go to Nineveh might well lead to disaster for Israel. Perhaps if he did not go, God actually would destroy the Assyrian capital and the threat along with it. But could he possibly disobey the Lord so directly? He may also have dreaded the personal consequences to himself if he, as a Hebrew foreigner, tried to approach the Assyrians with such an unwelcome message.

As it turns out Jonah's fear of Assyria was well-founded. Within about 40 years of his time, the pagans actually did invade Israel and carried the northern Hebrew kingdom into captivity in 722 B.C. The ten northern tribes were then referred to as "lost" although they eventually came back into Israel along with the captives from Judah under King Cyrus and his successors. The book of James in the New Testament is addressed "to the twelve tribes of Israel". The ten tribes were not lost in the sense of one's losing some object but in the sense of being captured and deported in a decisive battle.

Jonah's reluctance might also have been partly based on the fact that there was no such thing as a missionary to the Gentiles up to that time. The whole of the Old Covenant was more inward facing than outward facing. The general word of the Lord to Israel was "come up to Jerusalem" and "be separate from the nations" rather than as in the New Covenant, "go into all the world". One was born into the chosen people. While they were commanded to be kind to their neighbors and to be just in all their dealings with the Gentiles, they really did not seek converts. Thus Jonah's commission ran contrary to normal operations under the Mosaic law and simply had no precedent.

Nevertheless, from God's point of view, Jonah's reluctance was simple disobedience and the Lord set about to bring His servant back into His will.

The Fish That Caught A Man

Fleeing from an omniscient God is not easy. Jonah tried to escape by hiding himself in the bottom of the lowest hold on a Phoenician merchant vessel departing from Joppa.

The ship set sail and headed westward in the vast Mediterranean.

And then the Lord made His move. A disastrous storm came up which completely confounded the experienced Phoenician seamen. Seasoned as they were to the hazards of the Mediterranean, the sailors simply could not cope with the storm. They were very religious men, and when all else had failed, they tried to muster the crew and the passengers to pray to their respective gods. One would have expected to find quite a few gods represented on an international sea-going vessel of the times.

The guilt-ridden Jonah was one of those they asked to pray. When the prayers failed to get results, the seamen threw lots and determined that the problem was associated with the sulking Hebrew in the hold. They interrogated Jonah as to his spiritual persuasions and he spoke up about the Lord God of Israel, Creator of heaven and earth. There

Ultimately the Phoenician seamen had to act on Jonah's suggestion.

was something in Jonah's message that made the sailors respect the Hebrew.

They jettisoned the heavy cargo and tried desperately to right the ship into the wind and bring it to port. The storm grew worse, however, and all their efforts were unsuccessful. A miserable Jonah finally came to them and said that the only way they could save themselves and the ship was to cast him into the ocean.

What a transformation had taken place! Jonah, reluctant to go to witness for the Lord in a Gentile country, now found himself testifying before a group of Gentile sailors. Obviously, in confessing that his was the God who made the storm, Jonah was giving a powerful witness for that God. More than that, he was willing to sacrifice himself in order to bring deliverance to those Gentile pagans. The prophet was beginning to come into the will of God.

Now the crew reasoned that if the great God of Jonah could bring about such a terrible storm, what would that same God do to them if they harmed His prophet? Trying to save Jonah and themselves, they fought on. Only reluctantly they decided that the only way to preserve the ship was to try Jonah's advice and throw him overboard into the churning deep. They did so and the storm stopped immediately, as quickly as it came. The waters calmed and the skies turned blue with bright sunshine. The Phoenician crew, who had heard the word of the Lord from Jonah, had now seen the display of God's might and power. They bowed their heads in worship.

Even in his disobedience, Jonah had brought Gentiles to faith in the God of Israel. But his troubles were only beginning. He sank deep into the depths of the Mediterranean Sea. In his saga he tells of how he was surrounded by seaweed and it appeared that he would drown amidst the strange shapes on the ocean floor.

Suddenly, there was an unpredictable event. God provided

a great fish to save His prophet. Popular tradition has it that a whale swallowed Jonah, probably because the whale is the largest sea creature. Biblical accuracy, though, would require a real fish and it's quite probable that Jonah's extraordinary fish was especially provided by God for this purpose. Even the largest whale does not have a digestive tract that would accommodate a human being. Such biblical miracles, like the sun standing still and the parting of the Red Sea, have to be taken as supernatural acts on God's part and not rationalized.

In any case, it was a changed Jonah whom the fish vomited up on the beach. Three days and three nights is a long time to spend in the belly of a fish, and he apparently reconsidered the whole matter of his call to preach God's message to Nineveh. He found himself ready, willing and nominally able to fulfill the original command.

The Successful Missionary

Nineveh stood on the east bank of the Tigris River more than 500 miles from Israel. It was an arduous journey but Jonah fulfilled his mission to the letter. He preached the warning of the imminent destruction of the city in plain words — "Yet 40 days and Nineveh will be destroyed" (Jonah 3:4).

To his own amazement the entire city instantly accepted his message and became totally repentant. Everyone from the king to the lowest subjects repented before the God of Israel and covered themselves with sack-cloth and ashes. Even the livestock were covered as a sign of the intense repentance of the whole city.

How could it be? Jonah probably wondered. And we might well wonder with him. First of all, the Spirit of God was undoubtedly working on the hearts of the people. However, there is also a tradition about how the circumstances might have been used by the Lord to bring about this unexpected transformation. People saw Jonah making his way from the beach and toward Nineveh, and they ran ahead of him to tell of the miracle of a man who had come out of a fish. Jonah was perhaps stained and disfigured by the gastric juices and must have attracted much attention. If we bear in mind that one of the major deities of Nineveh was the fish-god Dagon, the prophet might have been already perceived as a man with a divine message before he ever arrived. God's extraordinary demonstration starts to make sense considering the disposition of the audience spiritually. Whatever the cause and effect, the city was totally responsive to Jonah's message and placed itself at the mercy of God.

And in His mercy, God did not destroy the Assyrian capital. But now Jonah was disappointed. Having finally repented enough to accomplish the mission, Jonah might have at least rejoiced in its success, but in truth he was not concerned about the welfare of the unbelievers.

The message to us in our day seems to be that although we live in a different age we have the same commission to share the word of God and the good news of Messiah to the whole world. We sometimes go in a different direction and we sometimes suffer for it. And perhaps we are guilty of not even rejoicing when our works show some success among the unbelievers. Many an excellent sermon has been delivered on the obtuse attitude and argumentative personality of Jonah.

Jonah And The Resurrection

But whatever the interpretations of the actual experiences of Jonah, there is a crucial meaning to the 3 days and 3 nights in the deep. The adventure makes him a type of the Messiah buried and resurrected, and Jesus Himself certified this emphatically in His teachings.

> "For just as Jonah was three days and three
> nights in the belly of the great fish, so shall the
> Son of man be three days and three nights in
> the heart of the earth." (Matt 12:40).

In Messiah's time the leadership of Israel searched for signs but they already had this remarkable one. Jesus' body would be in the earth for three days and three nights, He said. The miraculous experience of Jonah in the fish was a divine illustration of His own death, burial and resurrection. Everyone certainly knew the extraordinary story of Jonah and it is probable that many Jewish people were convinced and came to salvation once the resurrection was announced and the parallel was lived out.

The question arises of how the prophecy about three days and three nights was fulfilled since customary Christian teaching is that Jesus died on Friday and was resurrected on Sunday morning. By the western way of counting, this would only be one day or so and two nights, not three days and three nights. This in turn has led some interpreters to teach that Jesus had a Wednesday or Thursday crucifixion in order to allow 72 full hours before He was raised.

An argument for a Thursday crucifixion, and therefore a Wednesday evening Passover Seder, has been advanced from Palm Sunday. In Exodus 12:4 the Israelites were to take the lamb four days before Passover to examine it and see that it was without blemish. And so this argument says that when the Lord arrived on Sunday He gave the people four days before they would actually execute the sacrifice.

However, a Friday crucifixion can be understood in light of the Jewish way of calculating days, which is quite different than the western way. In the law for the circumcision of a male baby, eight days are to pass from the birth. According to the Jewish law, any part of a day before sundown is considered a full 24-hour day, and any time after sunset is also considered a full day. Therefore, if Jesus was buried before sunset on Friday and was raised from the dead anytime after sunset on Saturday (or Sunday morning), it would have fulfilled the Jewish conception of three days and three nights.

Most of the other passages in the gospels that deal with this question strongly suggest a Friday crucifixion. For instance, Luke 23:54 states that the body of Jesus had to be buried before the beginning of the Sabbath, which must have meant on Friday before sunset (it has been argued that the term "Sabbath" can refer to a feast day other than the customary Saturday Sabbath, but in such usage it is usually qualified so that it is clear that it is not referring to a Saturday Sabbath. The expression might be a "Day of Atonement Sabbath" or "Passover Sabbath day". It would be a rare usage of the term "Sabbath" by itself to refer to a holiday.)

John 19:31 states that this was a High Sabbath and some have interpreted this as meaning a festival day. However, the term High Sabbath is used in rabbinic literature to refer to a Saturday that occurs during a festival period, such as during the Passover and Unleavened Bread days. That would have been the case with the Saturday during the time of the burial of Christ because it fell during the Passover week.

Furthermore, the Lord predicted that when He died He would be raised from the dead "on the third day" (Matt. 16:21). If instead His body had to be in the grave for three full 24-hour periods then He would have arisen on the fourth day after His burial. The "third day" expression is satisfied if He were buried on Friday afternoon and raised on Sunday morning. We might liken to this parlance the English expression "on the day after tomorrow," in which we make reference to three different days.

After all of these complexities it must be admitted that the question may never be answered to everyone's satisfaction. The conclusion is that the day on which Jesus died is not nearly so important as the fact of why He died and the fact that He rose from the dead. But stress should be laid on the idea that Jewish Scriptures are best interpreted with Jewish rules of interpretation. In the kingdom to come the Lord may be asked this particular question many times.

Jonah, A Type

Jonah's pristine moment as a type of the Messiah is the three days and three nights, of course. Had Jesus not made reference to it, it might be argumentative, but the Lord Himself called it "a sign". (Matt. 12:38-39)

Further, there is tempting symbolism in the fact of Jonah ultimately taking the word of God to Gentiles, first a few on the ship and then a great city out in a foreign empire. In like manner the Lord, Who said, "I am come only unto the lost sheep of the house of Israel" (Matt. 10:5,6) inspired faith in a few Gentiles at first (the Syro-Phoenician woman, the servant of the officer, the centurion at the cross). Later, the word of God through Christ reached out to many a great city in distant empires.

Also the character of the particular message was the same. Jonah came warning of a judgment for sin. And the Messiah's mission is ultimately to save us from the impending day of judgment.

Finally, in one of Jonah's finest moments he acted very like the Lord. He was willing to sacrifice himself to save the others when the storm came up.

7

Micah

מיכה

A *Roman soldier disembarks from a galley ship that has docked at Caesarea, the Roman provincial capital of the province variously called Israel, Palestine, and Judea. He carries an official scroll with the seal of Emperor Caesar Augustus. The document is given to a representative of King Herod, who then reads it and hands it to an aide to have it publicly posted as a proclamation to the entire population of Judea.*

The decree from the Emperor in Rome is for a tax enrollment program for all citizens of the Empire, including Israel. The terms are difficult. Everyone is required to register for this taxation at their ancestral city, however far away they have been moved. In this manner no one will be missed.

There are to be no exceptions to Caesar's proclamation.

Bethlehem And Caesar's Decree

Although Caesar must have thought his tax reformation plan was his own idea, it was probably the Lord's. God had made Himself a puzzle of Messianic prophecy and needed cooperation betwen Caesar in Rome and the little village of Bethlehem some 5 miles south of Jerusalem. Those two became bound together in the central event of the story of mankind, the incarnation of Jesus Christ.

Some seven centuries before the time of the Messiah the prophet Micah uttered a simple and pointed prediction that is clear beyond all doubt:

> "But you, Bethlehem Ephrathah, though you
> are little among the thousands of Judah, yet out
> of you shall come forth to Me the One to be
> ruler in Israel, whose goings forth have been
> from of old, from everlasting." (Micah 5:2)

One might have expected that the ultimate ruler of Israel might come from the capital city, Jerusalem, but Bethlehem is not altogether unknown in the biblical revelation. After all, the Messiah was to be the son of David and King David was born to the shepherd family of Jesse in Bethlehem a thousand years before Christ. Also, the very name of Bethlehem is significant in terms of the Messiah's teachings. Bethlehem in Hebrew is *bet lechem*, which means "home of bread". It is one of those stray points of Scripture's pinpoint accuracy that the Messiah was to be called the "Bread of Life," and would say in His climactic moment, "This bread is my body."

For the earthly mother of Messiah, God chose the young Jewish maiden, Mary, who was engaged to Joseph, a Galilean carpenter. They lived with their respective families in the town of Nazareth in Galilee. The fullness of times had come and the stage was set for the long awaited arrival of the prophesied Messiah.

But Joseph and Mary were over 70 miles away from Bethlehem and, of course, she was in the final stages of her pregnancy. The Roman decree could not have come at a worse time, in their view. But there was no avoiding the will of the occupational government.

Considering the various angelic appearances involved with the birth of Jesus it would not have been strange for an angel simply to instruct the young couple to travel to Bethlehem for the birth. But God involved Caesar. Across the great sea, some 1,400 miles away from Judea, the Roman emperor provided the solution.

The Romans had raised the craft of government to a high level of efficiency, and taxation to an art form. Indeed the population of the empire received something for their taxes in the way of excellent roads, enthusiastic police and armies, and respected citizenship in the empire that dictated life and death to the known world. Caesar's plan seems to have been intended to close loopholes in far-flung provinces of the empire. People may have been avoiding taxes simply because the Roman government didn't know who or where they were. A census-type enrollment, involving home precincts and every single taxpayer, was put in place all over the empire.

It should be appreciated that people everywhere had moved away from the towns of their ancestral origin and the decree came as a hardship to a great many. Judea must have been a convenient province for the Romans to exercise their scheme because people knew their genealogical origins, inasmuch as this was a matter of the Jewish religion. The plan probably came closest to assuring that everyone was registered until the days of social security numbers and computers.

Naturally Caesar didn't know or care about the Jewish Scriptures or Messianic prophecy. We have met unbiblical personalities throughout the Scriptures who did respect the veracity of the Jewish Bible, such as the Pharaoh of the Exodus and King Herod, but Caesar Augustus was not among them. The idea of a Jewish deliverer probably wouldn't have troubled him. But just the same, he unwittingly arranged for the true king of Israel and the world to be born in the precise location the prophet Micah had specified. Joseph and Mary could not resist his order and prophecy marched on.

Ancient And Modern Bethlehem

The chosen couple may at first have grumbled when the decree was posted. What a difficult development this was. Mary was very close to giving birth and she would have to travel on a donkey, and even on foot, all that distance through difficult terrain.

There were two primary ways to go from Galilee to Judea in that day, and they are still the preferred routes. One was through the Samaritan mountainside, which was more direct, but it involved going up and down the numerous hills of the central Israeli topography. Mountain ranges and waterless stretches of wilderness made the route problematical. Also, the Jewish people were reluctant to travel through the Samaritan territories since there was a strong antipathy between Jews and Samaritans. Today's situation, with part of Samaria comprising the contested West Bank, presents a like situation some 19 centuries later. The other route involved travelling the Valley of Jezreel to the Jordan Valley, which descended down to the level of 1,200 feet below sea level near Jericho. The ascension to Jerusalem would take the couple to 2,500 feet *above* sea level, a difficult climb in some 35 miles. They would then travel a few miles south to the village of Bethlehem from Jerusalem.

Under ideal circumstances it would take over a week to make the trip. Taking a teenage girl nearly 9 months pregnant with her first child was not the ideal circumstance.

However, Joseph and Mary may well have realized that the imperial decree was all part of the divine plan for the birth of their unique child. It's altogether possible that they had also read the prophet Micah and, of course, they had already enjoyed the information of angels. The Roman

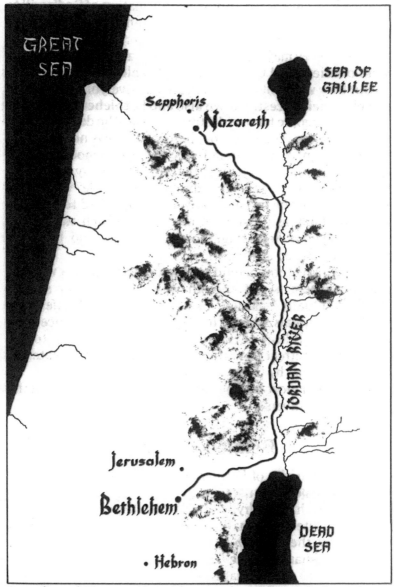

Joseph and Mary undertook an arduous journey in order to
fulfill Micah's prophecy.

avarice may have acted only as a confirmation of God's will to the favored couple. Possibly they felt entirely protected by God and honored to be in the center of His will, and therefore, they may have welcomed the task. In any case they were obedient and they set out for Bethlehem at once.

But they were not alone on the roads. Everyone else had to travel to their ancestral town also and Bethlehem, settled by the Jewish people for over 1,000 years, was the destination of many travelers. The little shepherd village was not exactly a tourist haven, and it offered very few accommodations for those who came. It's possible that there was only one inn in the town and it was already full of people who were registering for the census. Mary and Joseph had to be made as comfortable as possible in the stable, which was a cave where travelers kept their horses, donkeys and livestock while they stayed at the inn.

Though Westerners tend to think of a stable as a wooden building, there is not enough wood in Israel for such a luxury. Actually, natural caves are cool and safe from predatory animals when a fire is built at the entrance. The shepherds still keep their animals in caves in Israel today. This natural retreat from the unforgiving desert climate has always seen use by those who know the territory.

But it was a most humble circumstance for the birth of the King of the universe.

Bethlehem Today

The modern city of Bethlehem is in stark contrast to the humble village of Jesus' time. It's leading industry today is tourism, not husbandry, and it is a beehive of activity. The traditional site of the manger, certainly open to question, is covered by the Church of the Nativity. This remarkable building is shared by the Greek Orthodox, Roman Catholic and Armenian denominations. They literally each have an area within the structure and they conduct their own kind of worship in their own area. American Christian tourists are bewildered by this polyglot remembrance of the Messiah and sometimes put off by all the alien ritual.

It was always a place of controversy. The Bethlehem church has survived many conflicts, including the Crimean war of the last century, as different sorts of Christians sought to control the origin of their faith. In its earlier days the church would be invaded by horsemen who actually rode through the place swinging swords and making tremendous devastation at the site of the birth of the Prince of Peace. Finally the doorway was made so low and narrow that one person at a time had to enter by stooping, and so it is today.

Original mosaic floors reaching back to the fourth century grace the sub-structure of the present building, and the birthplace of the Messiah is enshrined in a natural cave in the basement. The "Nativity Scene" would surprise most Americans. There is no manger or figures of the family, the wise men, shepherds, etc., that are associated with Western Christmas versions. Rather the cave area is bedecked with silver censors of incense hanging from the ceiling and a prominent silver star that marks the site of the birth. The star may make reference to the star which led the wise men to Bethlehem and indeed, stars are a theme on the churches throughout the town.

The remarkable decor of the manger cave, or the birth cave, is out of the Greek Orthodox tradition since that denomination controls that part of the building. Some Christian pilgrims are disappointed in the difference between what they see and what they have always pictured as the birthplace of the Lord, but others stress the internationality of the Christian faith. In any case, the event and its setting are certainly not forgotten in the little town of Bethlehem.

The Magi

At the time of the birth of Messiah the religious leaders of Israel were educated in the Scriptures and they were fully aware that when the Messiah came He would certainly be born in Bethlehem. The visit of the Magi, or wisemen from Mesopotamia, who showed up in the capital city of Jerusalem just at the time of the birth makes this clear. These religious Gentiles had been exposed to Messianic prophecy, possibly from the Old Testament Scriptures distributed by Jewish people in Mesopotamia since the time of the Babylonian captivity. They fully expected, as biblical believers, the coming of the One who would be the "King of the Jews". More importantly, they understood that the King of the Jews is the King of all.

They were students of the stars, a part of the religious tradition of Mesopotamia, and they studied the skies tirelessly. If God indeed arranged the heavenly bodies "for signs and for seasons" as the book of Genesis attests, then the Magi used them in just that way. They took note of an unusual star that appeared a short time previous to the birth of Christ and they interpreted it as a sign of the coming of the King of the Jews. Stimulated by the Messianic prophecies and the unique astronomical events, these biblically learned Gentiles felt compelled to make a trip of some four or five hundred miles to Judea. Not having a perfect knowledge of the geography of the land of the Jews, the Magi went directly to the capital city, Jerusalem. There in an audience with King Herod, they would learn more exactly where the prophesied king could be found.

They evidently were of considerable stature because they were readily accepted at the palace and received graciously by Herod. Like Pharaoh before him, Herod had an appreciation of the accuracy of Scripture, especially where it concerned the birth of the Jewish deliverer. His interest was less than spiritual, of course, but he was impressed that the Magi had come and he sent his rabbinical scribes to investigate the prophecy.

It was not difficult for the scholars to cite that clear and highly specific statement of Micah, quoted above.

King Herod played the role of an interested observer, excited as were the Magi about the birth of the Messiah. He told them he wanted them to continue their quest for the child in Bethlehem, and as soon as they located Him, to let him know His whereabouts so that he, King Herod, could come to honor Him also.

The paranoid king was an assasin of considerable experience, having eliminated any number of competitive pretenders, and finally even his own wives, brothers, and sons in order to hold his throne. One can well imagine his opinion of the arrival of some Messianic figure who could well threaten his own rule. The Magi continued on their journey with the blessings of the king, but they were not to report back to him after all. The remarkable star continued to guide those who were inspired to come, and when they found Jesus with Joseph and Mary, they delivered the gifts they had brought for Him. Gold, incense and perfume from the East were rare and costly presents indeed, and the humble carpenter family must have been exceedingly honored to receive their resplendent guests. The remarkable visit was yet another confirmation of the divine reality of the birth of the Jewish Messiah.

Then the Lord warned the Magi in a dream not to return to King Herod with any information. They went back to Mesopotamia instead, using a route that did not pass through Jerusalem. But the chosen family was to confront still other troubles.

An angel warned Joseph to leave Bethlehem immediately and to flee to Egypt out of the reach of the king in Jerusalem.

Funds were provided for this journey by the Magi. It seemed that Herod had totally lost control in his jealousy and fear and he now undertook to slaughter the entire infant male population of Bethlehem. Not knowing the location of the Messiah-child or when he had been born, he issued an order to his soldiers to kill all the boys under two years of age in the town. In an echo of the story of Pharaoh's horrible infanticide at the time of the birth of Moses, the tragic massacre occurred, but the infant Jesus was safely dwelling in Egypt until the time He would return to the chosen nation.

Thus the Lord fulfilled, in a curious way, a statement of the prophet Hosea:

> "When Israel was a child, I loved him, and out of Egypt I called My son." (Hosea 11:1)

> "And was there until the death of Herod, that it might be fulfilled which was spoken by the Lord through the prophet, saying, 'Out of Egypt I called My son.' " (Matthew 2:15)

Ruler From Eternity Past

Micah's prophecy certainly identifies the Messiah as a human being issuing from a human birth at a specific time in human events. However, in the same statement the revelation is made that the Messiah has lived "from everlasting".

The Scriptures indicate that human beings commence at the time of conception and birth and not out of some sort of past lives or previous times. But the Messiah has lived forever; Jesus is a human being but always existed. The terminology indicates the deity of the Messiah since God is the only being in the universe who has existed from all eternity.

The virgin birth supplies the agency by which a human being can have existed previous to Adam and his sin nature. If Messiah had had a natural birth with a father and mother, He would be tainted with that same sin nature that all of us following Adam have inherited. But Messiah's humanity was not contaminated with this sin nature. The virgin birth enabled Almighty God to clothe Himself with human flesh and become a man but without that universal problem of the curse of Adam. We will deal with this point further in our chapter on Jeremiah.

The situation of the virgin birth is given in all of the four Gospels, either implicitly or explicitly. Luke, the physician, writes in detail, possibly indicating a close consultative relationship with Mary who, he said, "treasured all these things in her heart." He revealed that Mary was engaged to Joseph but not married as yet. She was a virgin and Luke frankly relates that Joseph was very surprised by her pregnancy at first. The angel's explanation taken together with the virgin birth prophecy (Isa. 7:14) persuaded Joseph to take Mary as his wife and adopt the miraculous child.

Luke's very specific recounting of the events may have been intended to confront those who cast aspersion on the birth and early life of Jesus. The absolutely unique event of the virgin birth solves many an implicit prophetic statement of the Old Testament, having to do especially with the "seed promise" prophecies. The unprecedented event amounted to an ingenious way for God to fulfill another of His most enigmatic prophecies.

Thus God brought together various prophecies of the Messiah in one elegant act. Micah's modest contribution, the place of that singular birth, was vital. We can imagine many pretenders to the office of Messiah being defeated on the point of their birthplace.

And once a prophet of God has spoken, Caesar himself must cooperate in the fulfillment!

8

Isaiah
ישעיה

*T*he prophet Isaiah, dressed in his priestly garments, is watching a herd of sheep. Most of them mill about the shepherd but occasionally some walk off by themselves and have to be called back.

Isaiah observes a shepherd busy shearing the wool off of an uncomplaining animal. The sheep stands quiet without resistance as his wool is being removed. The narrator reads from one of Isaiah's most inspired prophecies:

> *"All we like sheep have gone astray; we have turned, every one, to his own way; and the Lord has laid on Him the iniquity of us all.*
>
> *He was oppressed and He was afflicted, yet He opened not His mouth; He was led as a lamb to the slaughter, and as a sheep before its shearers is silent, so He opened not His mouth." (Isaiah 53:6-7)*

The Suffering Servant

Isaiah brought out more than any other prophet the suffering of the Messiah of Israel. His famous 53rd chapter, often referred to as the story of the "suffering servant", describes in great detail the sacrificial mission of the Messiah. The New Testament quotes it and alludes to it numerous times and it is regarded as one of the greatest proofs from the Old Testament that the Messiah would have to suffer and die in order to make atonement for Israel and the world.

Isaiah pictured the Messiah as an innocent lamb led to the shearers and to the slaughter. He would not put up resistance but would willingly offer Himself as a sacrifice for sin. This role of the Messiah is in contrast to Isaiah's other pictures of the Promised One as the King of Israel, triumphant in His kingdom. It was very important for the people to realize this dual role accomplished by the Messiah in two comings.

John the Baptist picked up on the theme when the time came for him to introduce the Messiah to Israel. He accomplished this vital task by referring to Isaiah's conception of Messiah as the Lamb:

> "The next day John saw Jesus coming toward
> him, and said, 'Behold, the Lamb of God who
> takes away the sin of the world!' " (John 1:29)

It's an amazing statement. A man approaches and John calls him "the Lamb", which is understood by the Jewish audience there at the baptismal site to be a sacrifice. And then John announced that this particular lamb takes away not merely the sins of Israel but the sins of the whole world.

Jesus characterized the unresisting lamb at the time of His arrest and trial. There is a difference between the way various animals react to certain treatment. Lambs respond quite differently from goats when they go to the slaughterhouse. They are quiet and receptive to their treatment. But goats are obstinate all the way, bleating and balking as they are taken.

The Messiah, as He stood before the High Priest of Israel, heard every sort of testimony and witness against Him but He didn't open His mouth to defend Himself. He spoke only when the High Priest confronted Him with the question, "Are you the Messiah?" And to that He responded, "I am." In His trial before Pontius Pilate, the Roman procurator, He responded only to the question, "Are you a king?". He therefore affirmed the key inquiries of both Israel and the world but He offered no resistance or defense to the charges.

Isaiah's precision is remarkable when he writes about Messiah's sacrificial mission. The following list of characteristics of the suffering servant and the reaction to Him by the people appear in Isaiah 53:

> He was despised and rejected by men.
> We considered Him punished by God.
> He was pierced for our transgressions.
> By His wounds we are healed.
> We have gone astray but the Lord has laid on
>   Him our iniquty.
> He was cut off from the land of the living.
> For the transgressions of my people was He
>   stricken.
> He was with the wicked and rich in His death.
> The Lord made His soul an offering for sin.
> He will prolong His days — the resurrection.
> He will justify many.
> He was numbered with the transgressors.
> He bore the sins of many.
> He made intercession for the transgressors.

It is almost as though Isaiah was an eyewitness to the events described in the Gospel accounts concerning the trial, death and resurrection of Jesus. Many who hear quotations from Isaiah 53 think that it is the New Testament that is being cited. This single chapter has probably led more Jews and Gentiles to accept Jesus as their savior than any other passage in the Old Testament Scriptures.

Hezekiah's Tunnel

Isaiah was not only a prophet but also a Levitical priest. He served in the great Temple of Solomon during the time of the Davidic monarchy in Judah, in the 8th century before

Christ. He served as court prophet to a variety of kings who differed particularly in their obedience to the Lord and His word. The Judean kings Uzziah, Jotham, Ahaz, and Hezekiah all enjoyed the counsel of Isaiah, but he was closer to Uzziah and Hezekiah, the more faithful kings.

A most fascinating find of the Jerusalem archeologists is the tunnel built by Hezekiah in the time of his association with Isaiah. It stands as a testimony of the engineering genius of antiquity. This tunnel is described in the Bible:

> "Moreover he provided cities for himself, and
> possessions of flocks and herds in abundance;
> for God had given him very much property.
>
> This same Hezekiah also stopped the water
> outlet of Upper Gihon, and brought water by
> tunnel to the west side of the city of David.
> Hezekiah prospered in all his works."
> (II Chronicles 32:29-30)

Isaiah must have frequented the tunnel often during its construction and when it was in service. The purpose of the tunnel was to bring the water supply from the Gihon spring, outside the city wall, into the protected area of the pool of Siloam. This was for convenience, but also for security during the times when Jerusalem was under siege by enemy armies. Water is crucial in the climate of Jerusalem. Hezekiah had good reason to fear that the Assyrians would attack and besiege his capital, and therefore he made this tunnel a top priority project for defense. With its primary water supply intact inside the city, Jerusalem could withstand a siege almost indefinitely.

Building a tunnel may seem to us a minor operation, with modern equipment and technology, but in ancient times the construction of a tunnel like this was a stupendous engineering feat. To make it work, the diggers

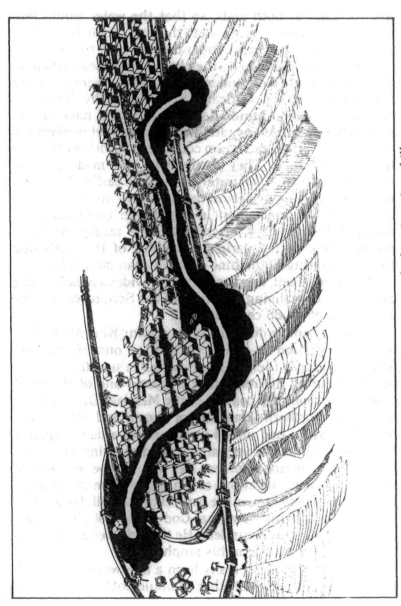

Hezekiah's tunnel was a marvel of engineering skill.
(For an interior view please see page 104)

had to begin at both ends, so that the water would flow smoothly from the spring area to the pool. There had to be a gentle decline in elevation from the spring to the pool.

Furthermore, of course, they had to meet somewhere in the middle in the dark underground. If they were off only a few degrees either vertically or horizontally, over the distance of several hundred feet, they would have missed each other by far. At any rate, when the tunnel workers got close to each other, each team could hear the other chiseling through the rock. They finally met and made a small adjustment so that the water could flow easily. The engineers were very excited about the success of this project, and they carved an inscription in the tunnel celebrating the accomplishment. This inscription, still readily readable, provides one of the earliest examples of the authentic Hebrew lettering of the time of the Judean monarchy.

The tunnel itself, needless to say, provides a breathtaking experience of realizing the truth of the Scriptures and the conditions of life 28 centuries ago!

Isaiah had a more difficult task in serving King Ahaz. Ahaz was characterized in the Scriptures as one of the very idolatrous kings of Jerusalem. However, a significant event occurred during his reign that triggered one of the great prophecies about the coming of the Messiah. During Ahaz' time, the northern kingdom of Israel and its Gentile neighbor, Syria, had joined in an unholy alliance against Judah. King Ahaz was very much afraid of an invasion from those two combined forces. He was in the process of examining the fortifications of Jerusalem when the prophet Isaiah approached him on the parapet of the wall. Isaiah gave Ahaz the comforting news that God would not allow Israel and Syria to destroy Jerusalem. He then challenged Ahaz to request a sign to confirm this prophecy.

Ahaz, who had never really been a follower of the Lord, responded with mock piety that he would not tempt the Lord

by asking for a sign. The prophet replied angrily that even if
Ahaz didn't ask for a sign, God was going to give him one,
and not to him only but to the entire dynasty of David. The
sign that the Lord would give the House of David was most
unusual:

> "Therefore the Lord Himself will give you a sign:
> Behold, the virgin shall conceive and bear a
> Son, and shall call His name Immanuel."
> (Isaiah 7:14)

The prophecy was that a virgin — *"ha-almah"* in the
Hebrew, would conceive and bear a son and his name would
be Immanuel, meaning "God with us". In the biblical
accounts, there have been several people who have miraculous origins, such as Adam, Eve, and Isaac, but no one had
been born of a virgin. This is the miraculous way in which
Messiah would enter the world, Isaiah announced. How
marvelously this was fulfilled when the young Jewish
peasant girl, Mary, conceived by the Spirit and gave birth to
the Holy One of Israel, the son of the Most High.

The Messiah And Galilee

While the prophets foretold that the Messiah would be
born in Bethlehem and would die in Jerusalem, Isaiah
predicted that much of Christ's work would be done in the
northern remote area of Galilee:

> "Nevertheless the gloom will not be upon her
> who is distressed, as when at first He lightly
> esteemed the land of Zebulun and the land of
> Naphtali, and afterward more heavily oppressed
> her, by the way of the sea, beyond the Jordan, in
> Galilee of the Gentiles.

> The people who walked in darkness have seen a
> great light; those who dwelt in the land of the
> shadow of death, upon them a light has
> shined." (Isaiah 9:1-2)

This would have seemed strange to many Israelites, especially those who lived in Jerusalem and often looked down upon Galilee as being an unspiritual backwoods area of the country. To say that the light of the Messiah would shine from Galilee would be to depart from God's workings in the past. One would expect the great teachings of the Bible to emanate from Jerusalem, where the Temple and the priesthood were, but not from the hinterlands of Galilee. That part of Israel was near Phoenicia and Syria, and was always influenced toward idolatry by those Gentile nations. In fact, the region was sometimes called the "Galilee of the Gentiles". The area was simply not respected by many of the people in the country, and it was considered an unclean, or unkosher, region.

We could readily understand if the Messiah were to choose Jerusalem, the capital city, as His headquarters during His ministry. But when Christ came, He utilized the town of Capernaum and the Sea of Galilee as His base of operations. The choice might seem strange but there are certain reasons why Jesus may have selected Galilee as the center of His ministry for some three years:

1) He was able to reach great multitudes by crossing over from one city to another by boat on the Sea of Galilee.

2) Galilee was a crossroads for people coming to attend the feasts in Jerusalem.

3) The common people were more receptive to His message than the heirarchy in Jerusalem.

4) The prophecy was fulfilled that the light
   would begin to shine from Galilee.

So Isaiah was vindicated once again and the Messiah saw
to it that the dawn of redemptive glory would begin to shine
in the quiet and beautiful Galilean countryside.

Titles Of The Messiah

One of the most beautiful passages in Isaiah's prophecy is
his prediction of the titles of the Messiah (Isaiah 9:6-7). Once
again we have the blending of the human and divine natures
in the personality of the Christ. The Messiah is spoken of as a
child that is born and a son that is given, yet this son has
titles that can be used only of the Creator: Wonderful
Counselor, Mighty God, Father of Eternity, and Prince of
Peace.

As a Wonderful Counselor, *"Pele Yoetz,"* the Lord meets
many of our most basic needs. Counselling has become a
profession today, but nobody ever counselled like Jesus.
Consider the episodes described by the Apostle John in his
third and fourth chapters. Nicodemus, a member of the
Sanhedrin, a teaching elder of the Israelites, went to see
Jesus by night. The Lord cut through all of the incidentals
and educated him on the realities of a spiritual new birth.
"You must be born again," Jesus said, with typical brevity
and force. Nicodemus never forgot that counselling session.
The woman in Samaria, who came to draw water from the
well, at first contended with the Messiah. She ran back into
town after talking with Jesus for a few minutes, however,
spiritually full to the brim with the living waters that the
Messiah gave to her. When Jesus taught the multitudes, He
did so in a way that the people had never heard before — with
divine authority. During the Sermon on the Mount, Jesus
frequently said "You have heard . . . but I say unto you." He

took the law of Moses and gave to it the powerful and godly interpretation it was intended to have.

He is also the Mighty God, *"El Gebor"*. Some regard Jesus as a great teacher or an outstanding religious leader, but Isaiah revealed that the Messiah is God the Creator Himself. The remarkable part is that the Creator has been willing to humble Himself, enter our history, and become a human being like us.

Another title Isaiah reveals is Father of Eternity, *"Avi Ad"*. This is sometimes translated Everlasting Father, but Father of Eternity seems to be a more accurate rendering. He is the Creator or Father of time and the creation, and He has existed for all eternity. It is certainly fitting that the Messiah should be called the Father of Eternity.

Finally, Isaiah refers to the Christ as the Prince of Peace, *"Sar Shalom"*. In so many ways He brings peace. The Messiah brings peace to the believer's heart when we receive Him and as we trust in Him day by day. It is the "peace that passes all understanding" and is truly understood only by those who have received the Lord and experienced it.

The Lord also brings peace between Jews and Gentiles in Christ, where the middle wall of partition is broken down (Ephesians 2). The law of the Old Covenant created a wall of enmity between Jews and Gentiles, but in Christ that wall is broken down and there is true peace.

The Messiah also brings peace within the body of Christ, as the Church fulfills its various ministries to its respective members, and to the community at large.

Finally, the Prince of Peace will bring peace to the whole world when He returns to the earth and establishes His kingdom of peace upon the earth. Righteousness will then cover the earth as the waters cover the sea and nations will not learn war anymore, in Isaiah's words.

Isaiah is sometimes called the Prince of the Prophets. His

is the most lengthy book of prophecy and it is something of a microcosm of the entire Bible. He captures with great poetic splendor both the judgments on the people of Israel and the great prophetic glory that awaits the entire world through the coming of the Messiah.

9

Jeremiah

ירמיה

T *he setting is in the Temple of God in Jerusalem around 600 B.C. Two prophets are having a debate. A large crowd of people are watching Jeremiah and Hananiah, both claiming to be bringing the word of God but delivering very different messages.*

Jeremiah has proclaimed that Jerusalem and the Temple would be destroyed by the Babylonian king, Nebuchadnezzar, and the people of Judah would be taken into captivity for 70 years. The message is melancholy, to say the least. Jeremiah is not a popular prophet. Hananiah, on the other hand, says that God will not allow His Holy City and His sanctuary to be destroyed but will rather protect His chosen people. Hananiah is more appreciated by the crowd.

Jeremiah is dramatizing his depressing message by wearing a wooden yoke around his neck, symbolizing the yoke that God is going to place on Israel. In dramatic defiance, Hananiah seizes the yoke and smashes it on the ground, symbolizing that the Lord will break Babylonia's yoke from off the people of Judah. Jeremiah shouts back that while Hananiah has broken the yoke of wood, God will fashion for Judah a yoke of iron which cannot be broken.

The Destruction

Nobody loved the city of Jerusalem and the Temple of God more than the prophet Jeremiah, who lived and ministered there. His difficult task was to prophesy the coming destruction of the city and the Temple, and he lived to see his prophecies vindicated. In 586 B.C. Nebuchadnezzar and the Babylonians threw down Solomon's magnificent Temple, destroyed Jerusalem and deported most of its population.

He was called the weeping prophet and Jeremiah was indeed a tragic figure. He wept just as the Messiah was to do so many centuries later over Jerusalem and its fate. Some of the people despised him because of his negative predictions and because he urged the people to submit to King Nebuchadnezzar, as this was the will of God. Ultimately he was to be tried as a traitor and jailed, only to witness the outcome of his every prediction from his cell.

It was so much easier to think of Jeremiah as simply a false prophet and to believe happier news like that given by Hananiah and others. We can imagine our own reaction if someone began to preach that our own nation would soon be destroyed and that we should submit to this fate. The outcry to silence Jeremiah became overwhelming and he finally was silenced. Of course, that had little effect on the will of God.

It was simply difficult for the people of Jerusalem to believe that God would forsake them after they had enjoyed His constant protection for almost four centuries. Was not Jerusalem the very home of Almighty God on earth, after all? Would the Almighty allow His chosen people to be captured and be taken into a pagan land? Jerusalem and the Temple had stood the test of time and the people fervently believed that it would survive an invasion from Babylon.

Jeremiah's appearance with the wooden yoke around his neck was obnoxious and offensive to those who had no conception that prophets really tell the word of God. Hananiah was, of course, expressing the will of the majority when he broke that wooden yoke and he probably received applause. But after consultation with the Lord, Jeremiah announced publicly to Hananiah that God's yoke would be a yoke of iron which could not be broken. God had had enough of the idolatry of Israel and the ritualistic nature of Temple worship. The Mosiac law had become corrupted beyond repentance, it seemed, and chastisement was to be the result. Thus, while the message of Jeremiah was terribly unpopular and apparently unpatriotic, it was the true word of God.

At Jeremiah's trial, the prosecution pressed for the death penalty. But an interesting mitigating circumstance was that the prophet Micah a hundred years earlier had also predicted the destruction of Jerusalem. Jeremiah was not alone in his woeful message, and perhaps those in the court had some respect for a prophet of God after all. The uneasy compromise was to imprison Jeremiah in a dungeon. The chosen people, like people of other nations everywhere, showed a true disregard for a message from God. Jeremiah is often compared to the Messiah Himself in the extreme frustration that attended his ministry.

Nebuchadnezzar and his armies arrived in 605 B.C. to beseige the city and deport various segments of the population. Another siege and deportation came about in 597, but in 586 it all came to a conclusion with a third and final attack on the city and the Temple. The people of Judah were carried away to Mesopotamia where they spent 70 years in captivity, a disaster also foreseen by Jeremiah:

"For thus says the Lord, 'When seventy years
have been completed for Babylon, I will visit you
and fulfill My good word to you, to bring you
back to this place. (Jeremiah 29:10)

In the ruins of Jerusalem the prophet composed the sorrowful book of Lamentations which expresses in exquisite poetry the grief of the Lord and His people over the ruin of the Holy City. The prophet's agony is complete:

"How lonely sits the city that was full of people!
How like a widow is she, who was great among
the nations! The princess among the provinces
has become a slave!

Nebuchadnezzar and the Babylonian army utterly destroyed Jerusalem and the Temple in 586 B.C.

She weeps bitterly in the night, her tears are on her cheeks; among all her lovers she has none to comfort her. All her friends have dealt treacherously with her; they have become her enemies." (Lamentations 1:1-2)

Annually, on the ninth day of the month of Av (August), the book of Lamentations is wept through its entirety by the chosen people. The commemoration, called Tisha B'Av, is done even today in modern Israel in memory of this 2,400 year-old tragedy.

Hope Of Return

God had not forsaken His people permanently, and through Jeremiah, He again announced to them their own future. The punishment was to be limited and Babylon in the end would pay for its sins as well.

"And this whole land shall be a desolation and an astonishment, and these nations shall serve the king of Babylon seventy years.

Then it will come to pass, when seventy years are completed, that I will punish the king of Babylon and that nation, the land of the Chaldeans, for their iniquity, says the Lord; and I will make it a perpetual desolation.

So I will bring on that land all My words which I have pronounced against it, all that is written in this book, which Jeremiah has prophesied concerning all the nations.

'(For many nations and great kings shall be served by them also; and I will repay them according to their deeds and according to the works of their own hands.)' "
(Jeremiah 25:11-14)

After 70 years in Babylon, the people of Judah would return to Jerusalem and rebuild their city and the Temple of God.

Jeremiah was given a chance to make a dramatic presentation of how firmly he believed in the fulfillment of his own prophecy. At the point when the Babylonians had already invaded Judah for the final time and had the countryside surrounding Jerusalem under their control, Jeremiah had a chance to purchase some land. With Jerusalem totally besieged, a relative of Jeremiah's approached him and said that there was a legal obligation for the prophet to purchase a parcel of family property in the town of Anathoth, a few miles north of Jerusalem. In the Law of Moses, land belongs to families and tribal delineations are kept very clear. Even under so extreme a situation as a siege by an invading army, Jeremiah's relative felt obligated to present the legal opportunity.

One might have expected Jeremiah to reject the offer immediately since Anathoth was already under Babylonian control. We can imagine that the land was not considered very valuable at such a time. Furthermore, was it not Jeremiah himself who had dutifully predicted that the entire kingdom of Judah would be wiped out and the people taken into captivity?

But Jeremiah proved to have as much faith in his predictions of the return as he did in the predictions of the destruction. He firmly believed that Judah would return from Babylon, and that family property would be continued and the Law of Moses would survive. Therefore he proclaimed in the most public manner that the Lord wanted him to buy the land, and he purchased the property. He made certain that the deed would be recorded so that when the people returned after the captivity his heirs would have ownership of the land. Faith like Jeremiah's was becoming rare in Judah.

On the subject of the restoration after the Babylonian captivity Jeremiah sounded an even more hopeful note. Looking far down the corridors of time he preached the ultimate future glory of Israel in the kingdom of the Messiah:

> "In those days and at that time I will cause to grow up to David a Branch of righteousness; He shall execute judgment and righteousness in the earth.
>
> In those days Judah will be saved, and Jerusalem will dwell safely. And this is the name by which she will be called: the Lord our Righteousness."

It is often the style of the Old Testament prophets to utter a message with a double fulfillment. Jeremiah's prediction of the return from Babylon was only the beginning of Israel's lasting redemption.

The weeping prophet is often remembered only for his difficult messages of destruction, but Jeremiah should also be remembered as a true prophet of hope. He backed up his unwavering belief in the word of God with action; he stood trial and went to prison and he even purchased a parcel of family property when it appeared that Judah was forever doomed. He announced in clear terms that his hope was not only in the return of the Jewish people from Babylon but in the blessings of Israel and the entire world when the true king comes into His kingdom.

The New Covenant

The Old Covenant seemed to be coming apart at the seams. People like Jeremiah might indeed respect property law and the other particulars of the Mosiac system but by and large, the people were simply not observing the Law of Moses. It certainly wasn't the fault of the Law, which was holy and righteous and good. The problem was that a worldly

people simply could not keep a holy law. The great defect in
the Old Covenant was with the *keepers* and not the Covenant
Maker. God was demonstrating to His chosen people and to
the world that the human race is sinful and desperately in
need of a new covenant and a savior. Neither they nor their
heirs were able to keep the Law and so the Old Covenant of
the Law of Moses was demonstrated to be an imperfect
relationship between God and man.

It was Jeremiah's task to announce that a New Covenant
was coming. The New Covenant would not be like the Old
Covenant in many significant aspects:

> "Behold, the days are coming," says the Lord,
> "When I will make a new covenant with the
> house of Israel and with the house of Judah —
>
> not according to the covenant that I made with
> their fathers in the day that I took them by the
> hand to bring them out of the land of Egypt, My
> covenant which they broke, though I was a
> husband to them," says the Lord.
>
> "But this is the covenant that I will make with
> the house of Israel: After those days, says the
> Lord, I will put My law in their minds, and write
> it on their hearts; and I will be their God, and
> they shall be My people.
>
> No more shall every man teach his neighbor,
> and every man his brother, saying, "Know the
> Lord, for they all shall know Me, from the least
> of them to the greatest of them," says the Lord.
> "For I will forgive their iniquity, and their sin I
> will remember no more." (Jeremiah 31:31-34)

It is important that when we speak of the Old Covenant we
realize that Jeremiah is referring specifically to the Law of
Moses and the covenant that God made with Israel at the

time of the Exodus from Egypt. The Lord is not referring to the Abrahamic Covenant, which continues in effect, and is not abrogated by the New Covenant. He specifically refers to the Old Covenant as the one made when God brought them out of Egypt, and which was written on tablets of stone. That Old Covenant required its adherents to teach others to know the Lord and to warn of the punishment of sin.

The New Covenant would be different. It was to be established by the Messiah Himself, and rather than the law being written on stone, the law of the Lord would be inscribed on the hearts of the believers in the New Covenant. Everyone under the control of the New Covenant would have a personal knowledge of the Lord, and would not need to be instructed to know Him. Furthermore, sin would be seen as forgiven, and punishment would not be a primary theme. The New Covenant was seen as a continuation of the grace revealed in the Abrahamic Covenant, which was only temporarily interrupted by the law concept of the Mosaic Covenant. (Galatians 3:17)

The New Testament gives the full revelation of how the New Covenant has been established. The Messiah Himself initiated the fulfillment of the New Covenant at His first coming. When Jesus was observing His final Passover before His death, He took the cup of wine and said, "This cup is the New Covenant in My blood, which is shed for you." (Luke 22:20). We who have trusted in Christ have entered into the New Covenant. The Lord has placed the law of His Spirit in our hearts, we all know the Lord as our Father, and our sins have been forgiven.

Thus Jeremiah prophesied that a New Covenant would come that would supercede the Old Covenant. The book of Hebrews confirms that the New Covenant has come and has been established. Actually, we are in the first stages of the New Covenant in the Church age. It will continue when the Lord returns and establishes His kingdom, and fulfills the New Covenant with regard to Israel and the Gentile peoples.

Curse of Jeconiah

Jeconiah (Coniah) was the last true king in Jerusalem who descended from the royal line of David. When he was captured in 597 B.C. and deported to Babylon by King Nebuchadnezzar, his relative, Zedekiah, was appointed to rule as a puppet king in his place.

Before Jeconiah was taken as a hostage to Babylon, Jeremiah frequently proclaimed the word of the Lord to him. Unfortunately he was one of the several idolatrous and evil kings in Judah's history. For 400 years the Davidic succession had ruled in Jerusalem — becoming one of the longest dynasties in human history. It was in stark contrast to the numerous brief dynasties who ruled in the northern kingdom of Israel, and in the Gentile nations. The longevity of David's dynasty stands as a testimony to the promise the Lord made David about never lacking a descendant to sit on the throne.

But now Judah was about to go into the Babylonian captivity. What would happen to the Davidic dynasty now? Jeremiah proclaimed that with Jeconiah, the reign of the royal seed-line from David over Jerusalem would come to a conclusion:

"Is this man Coniah a despised, broken idol? Is he a vessel in which is no pleasure? Why are they cast out, he and his descendants, and cast into a land which they do not know:?

"O earth, earth, earth, hear the word of the Lord!

> Thus says the Lord: Write this man down as childless, a man who shall not prosper in his days; for none of his descendants shall prosper, sitting on the throne of David, and ruling anymore in Judah." (Jeremiah 22:28-30)

There were several elements to this surprising and devastating prophecy. First, Jeconiah was to be considered childless. He had several sons, but from the standpoint of the monarchy, none of them ruled as Jeconiah's successor in Jerusalem. His seed would not prosper. This certainly was the case as Jeconiah's descendants witnessed the destruction of Jerusalem and its subjugation to Babylon. They went into captivity for 70 years, and this was the low point of Israel's history as a nation to that time. Furthermore, none of Jeconiah's descendants would sit upon the throne of David in Jerusalem.

So Jeremiah's declaration amounted to a curse upon the royal line of Jeconiah. After the Babylonian captivity, a descendant of Jeconiah, Zerubabel, was a leader of the returning pioneers, along with Joshua the High Priest. However, Zerubabel was not king over Jerusalem and neither he nor his descendants ruled as kings.

The effect this interruption of the royal line had on the political stability of Israel was negative enough, but there was also a serious impact on what had been revealed up to that point about the coming of the Messiah. God had already promised to David that his dynasty would last forever, and that the Messiah would be one of his descendants. So the Messiah has to be a descendant of David, but He must also be a legitimate heir to the throne of the Davidic monarchy. Therefore, He must be a descendant of David, have legal right to the throne, but not be tainted with the curse that was placed on Jeconiah and his descendants. How could all these specifications be accomplished? It was another puzzle that the Lord created for Himself with prophecies that were apparently contradictory.

God ingeniously solved the conundrum of Coniah through the virgin birth. In the special arrangements between the Lord, Joseph, Mary, and Jesus, Mary contributed something of significance to Jesus, but so did Joseph. As we see from the genealogy recorded in the Gospel of Luke, which is apparently Mary's genealogy, Mary is a descendant of David, but *not* through the royal line of Solomon and Jeconiah. Rather, she is a descendant of one of David's other sons, Nathan. She was the *physical* mother of Jesus, and so was able to pass the genealogy of David on to her son without any connection with the curse upon Jeconiah and his descendants.

However, the descendants of Nathan had no legal right to the throne. They were just cousins of the royal line that came from Solomon. It would not have been enough for Jesus merely to have avoided Jeconiah's curse. Joseph is very necessary to God's solution.

And here is where Joseph makes his contribution. Normally, Bible readers do not think so much about how important Joseph was in this whole situation. He was not the physical father of Christ and so his importance is sometimes overlooked. But Joseph's genealogy is given in the Gospel of Matthew and it is implicit that if Israel had been a monarchy at the time of the birth of Christ, and if there had not been a curse upon Jeconiah, Joseph, the humble carpenter of Nazareth, would have been the legal heir to the throne of David. Joseph would have been the king of Israel! (Please see page 118)

But Israel was not a monarchy. It was just a subject state to the Roman Empire, who had it's own appointed king, Herod the Great. So Joseph was a carpenter in Nazareth, and not a king in Jerusalem.

Nevertheless, he did have the legal right to the throne

and that is the point. When Joseph adopted Jesus, who had been conceived by the Holy Spirit and Mary, Joseph was able to confer upon Him the legal right to the throne of David.

So, through the agency of the virgin birth, Jesus was both a physical descendant of David through Mary and had the legal right to the throne through Joseph. But He was not corrupted with the curse of Jeconiah.

Jeremiah himself may well have been puzzled by the implications of his own prophecy of the curse. With hindsight we can all appreciate that the Lord was well in control as always.

A prophet in a difficult time, Jeremiah accomplished his difficult mission. He warned of God's judgment and he bore the punishment of speaking the truth. He urged upon his persecutors a message of hope of restoration. And finally he announced God's New Covenant, which is in force today. His ultimate pictures of Messiah's reign in the Kingdom to come await fulfillment in our own future.

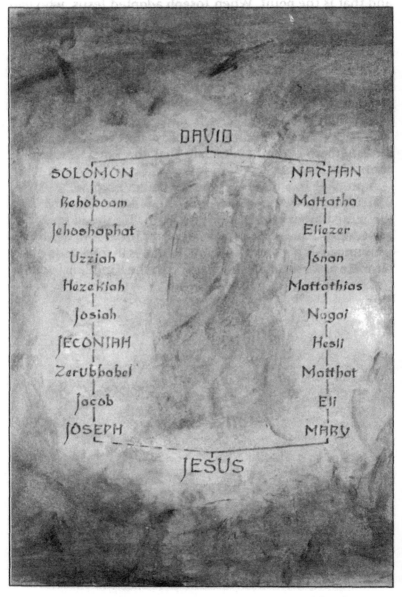

The major descendants of King David lead to
the Messiah through different family lines.

10

Daniel
דָּנִיֵּאל

A royal feast is in progress at the palace in Babylon when young King Belshazzar gets a sudden shock. High on the wall there suddenly appears an ominous message in luminous letters. The meaning is inexplicable to the king and his guests. He has sent for the aged Hebrew prophet Daniel to explain this strange apparition. Daniel glances at the Aramaic writing and slowly turns to Belshazzar to inform him that the Babylonian Empire has been judged by God and is at an end.

On that very night, the message of the handwriting on the wall is suddenly and completely fulfilled.

The Handwriting On The Wall

A disembodied hand had written in bold Aramaic, *MENE, MENE, TEKEL, UPHARSIN.* The guests at the royal gathering may have been a bit tipsy, since the wine was flowing freely that night, but they well understood that something spiritual was happening. In shock, they set down their glasses and cups, the very vessels from the Temple of the Lord in Jerusalem which had been plundered some 70 years before in Nebuchadnezzar's destruction of Jerusalem. The holy artifacts had been stored carefully in Babylon but now had been brought forth by the prideful Belshazzar as part of his entertainment.

The city of Babylon was under siege itself at the time of this party and it is thought that the festival was given by King Belshazzar as some kind of sign of bravado. The great army of the Medo-Persians was camped outside the city gates but the great walls of Babylon had so far held. The Babylonians were confident of their defensive ramparts and thought they could withstand a siege indefinitely. In defiance of the situation the king hosted this feast as though the Babylonians had won a victory.

If the guests thought at first that the startling effect of the handwriting on the wall was part of the king's plans for the evening, they were dissuaded by Belshazzar's fear. He was greatly upset at what he saw and he was shaking like a leaf. The Aramaic lettering was familiar to the crowd but the words used were cryptic. No one in the place understood the message. Finally it was remembered that Daniel had served King Nebuchadnezzar, Belshazzar's grandfather, in the matter of interpreting dreams. It was supposed that Daniel could bring some special wisdom to the king, and officers brought him to the scene.

Like his ancestor, Joseph, Daniel had the opportunity of giving to a pagan king a message from the God of Israel, and he fulfilled it:

> "This is the interpretation of each word. *MENE:* God has numbered your kingdom, and finished it;
>
> "*TEKEL:* You have been weighed in the balances, and found wanting;
>
> "*PERES* (single form of *UPHARSIN*): Your kingdom has been divided, and given to the Medes and Persians."
>
> Then Belshazzar gave the command, and they clothed Daniel with purple and put a chain of gold around his neck, and made a proclamation concerning him that he should be the third ruler in the kingdom. (Daniel 5:26-29)

Like Joseph, too, Daniel received a royal appointment in

Babylon was protected by mighty walls.

recognition of his spiritual knowledge. But to his relief he would never rule in Babylon because the kingdom fell before morning. That very night Darius the Mede and the combined armies of Medea and Persia penetrated the walls and overwhelmed the great city of Babylon. The event occurred in October of 539 B.C.

The aged Daniel had served the Babylonian court for about 66 years as an honored Hebrew deportee from the destruction of Jerusalem. He had been born and raised in Jerusalem as a member of the royal household there and he was a prince of the kingdom of Judah. When Nebuchadnezzar made his initial invasion of Judah and besieged the city of Jerusalem in 605 B.C. he took a number of prominent and intelligent citizens as hostages to his capital city of Babylon. Among those taken was the brilliant young prince, Daniel.

Nebuchadnezzar was a more enlightened conqueror than some others of ancient times. Where the Assyrian Empire pursued a policy of uprooting whole populations of conquered peoples, the Babylonians preferred to leave captured territories intact. Rather, Nebuchadnezzar's policy was to take young potential leaders from the nations which he overcame and see that they received training and education in Babylon. He might then send them back to their own countries to rule as his representatives.

Thus, young Daniel, probably a teenager at that time, received his education in the royal university of Babylon. Through divine providence he became a primary advisor to King Nebuchadnezzar himself. Since the ancient days of Joseph and Moses there was no more prominent Hebrew prophet in a Gentile court for 1,000 years.

It was Daniel's uncanny ability to interpret dreams, and the pagan appreciation of such spiritistic skills, that earned him his position. The Babylonians were very taken with the idea of wise men with special knowledge. But Daniel was superior to the most advanced magi of that nation.

During Daniel's training period Nebuchadnezzar experienced two dreams which his wise men could not interpret. One was of a great statue made of several different metals. It was destroyed by being hit by a stone. We will say more about this extraordinary dream below. The other dream was of a great tree that was chopped down, and Daniel interpreted this one as King Nebuchadnezzar himself being struck down with a disease called boanthropy. Indeed, the mighty ruler who had conquered vast empires disappeared from public view and experienced this debilitating illness exactly as Daniel had predicted. When he was restored to his senses after some seven years, he was converted at least to the understanding that the Lord God of Israel, whom Daniel worshipped, was in control of the destinies of the kings and kingdoms on earth.

Daniel's own visions gave him a very complete understanding of future world events and the ability to prophesy over vast periods. His visions of a succession of warring beasts, which he understood to mean the Gentile world powers from the Babylonian era to the second coming of Christ, is absolutely accurate. The kingdoms of Babylon, Persia, Greece and Rome came and went just as Daniel saw them, and we are still living in a derivative of the former Roman Empire.

After Nebuchadnezzar's reign the succession of kings is not completely clear but it is believed that Belshazzar was Nebuchadnezzar's grandson. Of course, the grand festival of defiance was his last act as king of Babylon. We still utilize the expression "the handwriting on the wall" to connote information about some portentous event.

The history in the book of Daniel is confirmed in other ancient writings, such as that of the Greek chronicler Herodotus. He corroborates that the Medo-Persian army used the strategy of diverting the Euphrates River, which flowed in conduits under the walls of Babylon. A temporary dam was built some distance upstream from the city and, at the moment of the diversion of the water, a platoon of troops was moved into the conduit behind the receding river and passed unseen to the inside of the city. Once there, they were able to open the gates and allow the entire army to invade. Herodotus confirms that the Persian soldiers discovered the people of Babylon in a drunken festival and there was practically no resistance. The entire description squares perfectly with that given by Daniel from the divine perspective.

God not only terminated the Babylonian Empire but also their captivity of the Hebrew people. As Jeremiah had prophesied, they had been in this foreign nation for some 70 years. Their Temple was in ruins in Jerusalem and many of the sacred vessels and implements of the Temple had been in storage in Babylon for all this time. Belshazzar's final act of idolatry and disrespect for the things of the Lord brought down his reign and his kingdom, and set in motion God's plan to bring the people of Judah back to Jerusalem. The fall of Babylon preceded the benevolent rule of the Persian king, Cyrus, who issued his famous decree for the Jewish people to return to Jerusalem to build the house of the Almighty God.

Darius and Cyrus are considered the same person by some historians, while others believe that Darius was Cyrus' chief commander of the Persian army. At any rate, they were closely associated at the time of the capture of Babylon and the establishment of the new world power, the vast Persian Empire.

Daniel had studied the book of Jeremiah and knew the length of the captivity in Babylon. He survived the entire time and saw the Word of God vindicated. It was a sterling example of the advantage of understanding biblical prophecy in living one's day-to-day existence.

The Statue—The Times Of The Gentiles

Nebuchadnezzar's dream of the statue was one of the most significant dreams in history. It occurred not long after Daniel had graduated from the royal university. It isn't clear whether or not Nebuchadnezzar remembered his dream or not. What is clear is that he was troubled by it.

He summoned all the learned counselors of his court but could not find an answer to his dilemma. He had forgotten the dream, or some of its details, and the significance of it was a mystery to him. In his anger over the ineptitude of the royal wise men he issued a death warrant for virtually all wise men in Babylon. Daniel would certainly have been affected by this decree, and when the official word reached him he asked for time to obtain the information from the omniscient God of Israel.

After asking his friends to pray with him, Daniel went before the Lord and asked for the revelation concerning the dreams of the king of Babylon. The answer was overwhelming. Nebuchadnezzar had dreamed nothing less than the political future of the entire times of the Gentiles, from Nebuchadnezzar's conquest of Jerusalem to the final reign of Messiah in the Kingdom to come.

In a sense, the era from Abraham to Daniel might be called "the times of Israel", from a biblical perspective. Certainly during the time of the Davidic monarchy Israel was perceived as a major world power and was entirely independent. But now the Babylonian captivity had terminated that independence. Throughout the rest of the history of this age, even to our own times, Israel would be subjugated to the power of the other nations. And thus the Messiah referred to these times as "the times of the Gentiles" (Luke 21:24). The Babylonian captivity lasted for the first 70 years, but even after the restoration of Israel the Jewish people remained

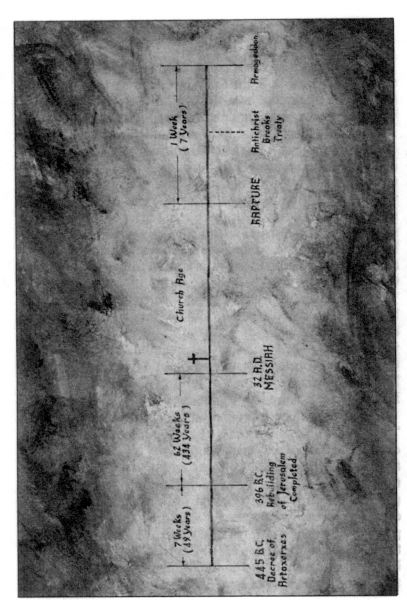

Daniel foresaw the coming of Messiah and the end of the age
in his remarkable "Seventy Weeks of Years" prophecy.

under the domination of the successive world empires. This situation will continue until the times of the Gentiles are completed at the second coming of Messiah, when world affairs will return to "the times of Israel" again. At His second coming the Lord will establish His own kingdom with Israel as the head of the nations and Jerusalem as His capital. All of this is depicted in the astonishing dream of Nebuchadnezzar:

> "You, O king, were watching; and behold, a
> great image! This great image, whose splendor
> was excellent, stood before you; and its form was
> awesome.
>
> "This image's head was of fine gold, its chest
> and arms of silver, its belly and thighs of bronze,
>
> "Its legs of iron, its feet partly of iron and partly
> of clay.
>
> "You watched while a stone was cut out without
> hands, which struck the image on its feet of iron
> and clay, and broke them in pieces.
>
> "Then the iron, the clay, the bronze, the silver,
> and the gold were crushed together, and became
> like chaff from the summer threshing floors; the
> wind carried them away so that no trace of them
> was found. And the stone that struck the image
> became a great mountain and filled the whole
> earth." (Daniel 2:31-35)

The statue in human form was composed of several metals at various stages of the body. The head was of gold, which represented the kingdom of Babylon and Nebuchadnezzar in all his glory. The chest and arms of silver represented the Medo-Persian Empire, which lasted from the sixth to the fourth century B.C. The stomach and thighs of brass stood for the Grecian Empire, lasting from the fourth to the first century B.C. The legs and feet were of iron at the top and a mixture of iron and clay at the toes. This mixture represented the Roman Empire that began in the first century B.C., and in a certain sense, continues to the present time The Roman Empire will be revitalized in the Tribulation period when a ten-nation confederacy of Europe will achieve power under the Antichrist. Thus Daniel's last empire is not yet finished but will rise to power again in the same location. Finally, the stone which is hurled as a missile against the feet of the statue and pulverizes the image represents the Messianic kingdom of God. In the dream, the stone grows and covers the whole earth, symbolizing the universal destruction of the kingdoms of the times of the Gentiles. Peace will come to humanity in permanent form at last when the kingdom of God is established on earth.

Thus, through a dream of a powerful monarch of his time, the prophet Daniel foresaw the framework of the rest of world history and revealed it to the king, and to us, in his book. The king was impressed that Daniel could tell him his dream, which he purported to have forgotten, but he would be extremely amazed if he could look at the outcome from our time. The kingdoms came and went exactly as Daniel prophesied and this fact has caused scholars who do not believe the Scriptures to theorize that the writer of the book of Daniel lived many centuries after Daniel's time. Once a person has decided there is no such thing as prophecy, he has a problem with accurate objective predictions such as Daniel's, and he has to shift the times of the author around. For believers of the Bible this is nothing more than complimentary. If one can't get around a prophecy other than changing the lifetime of the author by centuries, then it's a very good prophecy. There is certainly much evidence for the authenticity of Daniel's book and the fact of his living in Babylon in the times that he states.

We are convinced that God revealed the future for Daniel's time just as much of the Bible is still future to our own time. Just as Daniel's revelation about the times of the Gentiles came out exactly as prophesied so then will the Lord's revelation about things yet future come to pass.

The Seventy Weeks

One of Daniel's great motivations in life was the fact that the Jewish people would be able to go back to the land and restore the worship of God in Jerusalem. He himself would be too old to go back as a pioneer, into a situation much like pioneer Israel today. But his readings in Jeremiah had confirmed that Israel would be restored and he thrilled to that message.

He began to pray to the Lord about the restoration while acknowledging the sins and the idolatries of his people and their ancestors. His mind was filled with questions about what would come as the conclusion of the 70 years in Babylon was drawing near.

And at that point, God gave Daniel one of the most startling and detailed prophecies about the future of Israel in the entire Bible. The angel Gabriel appeared to the faithful prophet and made a new revelation about the number 70. This time it was not 70 years in Babylon, but 70 "sevens" concerning Israel and Jerusalem. The normal English translation is "weeks" but the angel was talking of "70 sets of 7". And the prophecy this time did not concern the times of the Gentiles and the succeeding world powers but Israel itself:

> "Seventy weeks are determined for your people
> and for your holy city, to finish the
> transgression, to make an end of sins, to make
> reconciliation for iniquity, to bring in

everlasting righteousness, to seal up vision and prophecy, and to anoint the Most Holy.

"Know therefore and understand, that from the going forth of the command to restore and build Jerusalem until Messiah the Prince, there shall be seven weeks and sixty-two weeks; the street shall be built again, and the wall, even in troublesome times.

"And after the sixty-two weeks Messiah shall be cut off, but not for Himself; and the people of the prince who is to come shall destroy the city and the sanctuary. The end of it shall be with a flood, and till the end of the war desolations are determined.

"Then he shall confirm a covenant with many for one week; but in the middle of the week he shall bring an end to sacrifice and offering. And on the wing of abominations shall be one who makes desolate, even until the consummation, which is determined, is poured out on the desolate." (Daniel 9:24-27)

The 70 weeks, therefore, were broken down into three periods: seven weeks, 62 weeks, and one week. The separate segments give the clue to what the sevens refer to. The prophecy states plainly that its starting point is the decree concerning the rebuilding of the city of Jerusalem, and the believer in the Bible of those ancient days could see this happen. It was to wait almost a century after Daniel's prophecy but a specific decree was given concerning rebuilding the city and its walls. This was in 445 B.C. in the time of Nehemiah. King Artaxerxes Longiminus (Neh. 2:7-9) issued such a decree in that year and it started the clock on Daniel's 70 sets of sevens.

Now that the beginning point was determined, it was necessary to understand the significance of the "weeks". The work of rebuilding the city, with its walls and streets, took about 49 years and was completed around 396 B.C. This period of time gave the key to the 70 weeks prophecy. If 7 weeks equalled 49 years then one week actually would equal 7 years. The weeks, or "sevens", in Daniel's prophecy were actually 70 weeks of 7 years each.

The 62 weeks of the next segment therefore, would be 62 times 7 years, or 434 years. Added to the 49 years already expired in the rebuilding of the city this would bring the prophecy to a total of 483 years from its beginning point in 445 B.C. Thus the end of the 69 week period, or 483 years from 445 B.C., would bring the fulfillment of the prophecy of the coming of Messiah the Prince to approximately 38 A.D. For all intents and purposes that is very close to when Jesus was conducting His public ministry. However, the prophecy is more precise than that. Biblical years are understood as containing 360 days rather than 365 for prophecy calculations. Utilizing those shorter years, the 483 years actually would end at around 30 A.D. Without burdensome calculations it is clear that the second segment, the promise of the coming of Messiah the Prince, who would be "cut off," very accurately identifies the time Christ presented Himself in the city of Jerusalem at the triumphal entry on Palm Sunday.

Readers are referred to Satan in the Sanctuary by the authors for very precise calculations that explain this prophecy down to the exact day. Sir Robert Anderson, an astronomer of the 19th century, computed Daniel's 69 weeks to lead precisely from the decree to restore and rebuild Jerusalem to Palm Sunday!

To recap that, the angel told Daniel of 70 "weeks", or 70 sets of 7 years, that would describe the future of Israel. The 70 weeks are broken up into segments and marked by key events. The start of the prophecy is established as the decree about rebuilding Jerusalem and the first 7 weeks, or 49 years, was the time in which that event was accomplished. In 62 more weeks the Messiah would be cut off, and then the city and the sanctuary would be destroyed. The first 69 of the 70 weeks of years are therefore clearly indicated by unmistakable events. The destruction of the city and the sanctuary, of course, happened in 70 A.D. under Titus and the Romans. Significantly, the prophecy establishes that Messiah was to come and be cut off before the destruction of the Temple, a disaster no one could miss.

The Seventieth Week

There is, of course, one week left to be fulfilled, or a period of 7 years. The death of the Messiah stopped the clock on Daniel's prophecy. In effect, a "time-out" was called and it has now lasted more than 19 centuries.

The clock will start again when the Antichrist ("the prince who is to come") makes a covenant with Israel, as is clear from the beginning of Daniel's final verse above. The false messiah and the nation of Israel have to make a treaty to initiate the final period of 7 years. We are persuaded that this event will not occur until after the Rapture of the Church, when Christ returns to take the believers out of the world. Some time after that the Antichrist will rise on the world scene and consummate the 7-year agreement with Israel. This counterfeit messiah will arise from the people who were responsible for the destruction of the second Temple in 70 A.D., the Romans. The Roman Empire will be revived in the end times and many think that the 10-nation confederacy, called the European Common Market, fulfills that part of the prophecy.

At any rate, the Antichrist will not appear at first to be an evil person but actually one who will have the capability of solving difficult world problems. In reality, however, he will be the enemy's man on the earth. He will deceive the world in general and Israel in particular. The contents of the treaty that the Antichrist will make with Israel are not revealed but we might speculate that it would contain guarantees for the protection of Israel's territorial rights. Also, it might specify an agreement to permit Israel to rebuild the Temple of God in Jerusalem. Sacrifices are mentioned in Daniel's final verse and that would require a Temple in the Tribulation period.

But the Antichrist will break the treaty with Israel at the mid-point of the agreement, or after 3½ years. He will commit "the abomination of desolation", which is described by the Apostle Paul in graphic detail:

> Let no one deceive you by any means; for the
> Day will not come unless the falling away
> comes first, and the man of sin is revealed, the
> son of perdition,
>
> who opposes and exalts himself above all that
> is called God or that is worshiped, so that he
> sits as God in the temple of God, showing
> himself that he is God. (II Thess. 2:3,4)

The Antichrist will actually claim to be God and will sit in the Temple in Jerusalem to receive the worship of Israel and the world. From this point to the end of the Tribulation there will be tremendous judgments falling down from heaven upon the earth. The book of Revelation, also specifying a 7-year period divided into two halves (Rev. 11:1-3, for example) gives the judgments. The Antichrist will gather together the armies of all the world to war against the Lord and against Israel. He will almost succeed in this mad final destruction. He will have destroyed much of Jerusalem, but at this lowest point in Israel's long and difficult history the Messiah will return and will defeat the enemies of the Promised Land. And so

Daniel's 70th week will end with the second coming of Christ. He will establish His kingdom upon the earth and will reign for 1,000 years.

Volumes have been written on the events of the final 7 years of tribulation. In the space available here we have only given the high points. Our purpose in this small book is to detail the Messianic prophecies, and of course, the 70 weeks is one of the great ones. When Daniel actually times out the period of Messiah's appearance on earth, he is giving a fact available from no other prophet. There were likely many people in Israel when Jesus came who received Him because the time was right. The 70 weeks prophecy is not really difficult to calculate. And of course, in all generations, sincere Jewish people were watching for Messiah.

With hindsight it is inspiring to see the accuracy of Daniel. We can rest assured that the 70th week will happen according to the details he gives.

The prophet lived a long and prayerful life outside the Promised Land but he could see so clearly the destiny of Israel, especially in regard to the Messiah. It is humbling to realize that some of the most vital of his 25 century-old predictions still await fulfillment in our own future.

11

Zechariah
זכריה

*A*n agitated figure bursts into the Temple courtyard surprising some of the leaders of the Sanhedrin who are conversing with one another. They recognize him as Judas, the follower of Jesus who they paid off to identify the Lord on the night of His arrest. Judas is distraught. His eyes are wild. He tries to hand back the bag of silver coins but the Sanhedrin members turn away. They refuse to take the blood money. Judas then hurls the bag to the floor of the courtyard and the coins splash out in all directions. He then turns and flees the scene. Wracked with remorse, he takes a rope and hangs himself over the cliff that looks down on the valley of Gehenna, on the south side of the Temple mount.

Judas And Zechariah

The story of Judas' betrayal of Jesus is one of the most familiar in the Bible. The very name of Judas is synonomous with treachery.

He had been with the Messiah and the other disciples for three years and was their intimate friend. He even was trusted with the treasury of the small band of itinerant believers in Christ. He had seen the miracles that the others had seen and he had heard all of the marvelous teachings of Jesus during His earthly ministry. We are not told his precise motivation but apparently he became disenchanted with both the method and the message of the Messiah.

Jesus did not fit Judas' concept of the Messiah and he evidently convinced himself that the best course of action for him was to cooperate with the leaders of Israel who wanted to arrest the Lord. Obviously, he didn't think he was dealing with the Son of God at all. Meeting secretly with the priests and members of the Sanhedrin who were opposed to Christ, he agreed to identify and deliver Jesus to them at a price of 30 pieces of silver. Certainly this is one of the most famous transactions in history. Everyone immediately is aware of the reference when we mention 30 pieces of silver.

Judas kept his part of the bargain and identified Jesus for the Temple police in the Garden of Gethsemane. Apparently the police didn't want to take Jesus while He was teaching publicly for fear of the crowds. And so it was important that a reliable witness identify the Galilean in the dark of night. With the infamous kiss of greeting on the cheek of our Lord, Judas accomplished his mission and earned his fee.

But as Jesus' trial progressed, things were not working out as Judas had anticipated. Judas may have thought that the Lord would merely be sentenced to prison but it appeared that He was to be executed instead. It began to dawn crushingly on Judas that he had "betrayed innocent blood". He was overwhelmed with remorse and suddenly he tried to undo the great damage he had done.

It is unlikely that this man, whom Jesus called the "son of perdition," actually repented in any true sense. But he obviously could not handle his guilt. To try to find some peace he attempted to return the money but those who had paid the bribe now refused to take it back. They called it "blood money" and it was unlawful for them to receive it for the Temple treasury. How sensitive they had become about the letter of religious law. Here the King of Glory was being tried for His life on trumped-up charges and the spiritual leaders were concerned about the receipt of tainted contributions. How typical this was of the teaching of the Lord concerning straining at a gnat and swallowing a camel.

The Temple officials must have been embarrassed over the unpleasant scene of Judas hurling the coins to the floor of the Temple courtyard, and they gathered up the money and put it in a special fund. Matthew informs us that it was eventually designated to purchase a parcel of ground in the valley of Hinnom, to be used for burying paupers. This was called the potter's field. The traditional site of the potter's field can be visited today in the Hinnom Valley, which was also called Gehenna. Jesus had referred to this place, which was a dumping ground for Jerusalem in which a perpetual fire burned, as literally hell on earth.

Though the above story is so familiar, few realize that the entire episode was prophesied some five centuries previously by the prophet Zechariah. Like some of the other prophets before him, such as Jeremiah and Ezekiel, Zechariah was commanded by the Lord to dramatize a scenario before the people. The prophets did not always use words but sometimes portrayed scenes for the interpretation of the onlookers. Zechariah was instructed to perform before the people like a shepherd with a staff. He was to ask for his wages as their faithful shepherd and, after some deliberation, they arrived at a price:

> Then I said to them, "If it is agreeable to you, give me my wages; and if not, refrain." So they weighed out for my wages thirty pieces of silver.
>
> And the Lord said to me, "Throw it to the potter" — that princely price they set on me. So I took the thirty pieces of silver and threw them into the house of the Lord for the potter.
> (Zech. 11:12-13)

What a small price! Thirty pieces of silver was an amount to be paid for a slave. The wage was actually an insult to a shepherd, but it expressed what the services of the good shepherd were considered worth to the nation of Israel. If there is sarcasm in the Bible, it is surely here. God describes the amount of the wages as "that princely price". It is with biting irony that the Almighty refers to the amount of the wages. Then the Lord told Zechariah to take the 30 pieces of silver and throw them to the potter in the House of the Lord. The command is rather strange since there were no potters in the Temple. It would be unlawful for such activity to take place in that sanctified setting. To find a potter one would need to go outside the Temple and into the marketplace of the city. Nevertheless, Zechariah dramatized exactly what he was told.

It was not until the time of the arrest of Jesus that Matthew and the disciples realized the significance of this subtle prophecy. The 30 pieces of silver that were used to pay for the betrayal of Jesus were indeed thrown into the Temple, and then later went to the unnamed potter to buy his field for the purpose of burial. It all came about just as Zechariah predicted. Those who had read and understood Zechariah's portrayal could now piece together the meaning of the drama. The nation had dreadfully undervalued its shepherd.

"Strike The Shepherd"

In the same context of the shepherd drama the Lord told Zechariah that if the shepherd was smitten, his sheep would scatter:

"Awake, O sword, against My Shepherd,
against the Man who is My Companion," says
the Lord of hosts. "Strike the Shepherd, and
the sheep will be scattered; then I will turn My
hand against the little ones. (Zech. 13:7)

In the visual drama by the prophet, Zechariah as the shepherd is struck, and indeed the sheep are scattered.

This is a portrayal of the fact that the Messiah, the ultimate Good Shepherd, would indeed be struck down and His sheep, the people, would go off in all directions. Jesus Himself quotes this incisive passage at the time of His arrest in the Garden of Gethsemane (Matt. 26:31). While Peter and the others, earlier that same evening, protested defensively at the Passover supper in the Upper Room that they would stand by Jesus to the end, the Messiah knew better. He knew that they all would disappear and that Peter himself would deny the Lord three times over before dawn the next day. In fact, by the time of the crucifixion, none of the disciples were anywhere to be found, with the possible exception of John and three of the women closely associated with the ministry. Peter had fulfilled the Lord's prophecy about the denials and all of the rest of the sheep were scattered to the four winds.

And so once again, the dramatic portrayal by the remarkable Zechariah was fulfilled in the divine scenario of the life and death of the Messiah. Until the resurrection and the new confidence it brought them, the sheep had scattered when the Shepherd was struck, exactly according to the prophecy.

Messiah, The Branch

Zechariah also made verbal prophecies, written in his book, in addition to his dramatic portrayals. Like Isaiah before him, Zechariah predicted a name for the Messiah:

> "Then speak to him, saying, 'Thus says the Lord of Hosts, saying: "Behold, the Man whose name is the BRANCH! From His place He shall branch out, and He shall build the temple of the Lord;" (Zech. 6:12)

This prophecy sounds curious indeed. The Messiah's name wasn't really "The Branch" but that nomenclature was associated with Him. Isaiah had already indicated that the

Messiah would be like a branch in that He would be a descendant from the family tree of Jesse and David (Isa. 11:1). But Zechariah's prophecy announced that "Branch" would be His name.

Matthew picked up on this theme. After King Herod's death, when Joseph and Mary saw that it was safe to bring the young infant back to Israel from Egypt, they did not settle in Bethlehem. Rather they went on to their original northern home in Galilee, Nazareth. The name of this small city struck Matthew as being the fulfillment of Zechariah's prophecy, for he understood the testimony of the prophet as indicating "he shall be called a Nazarene" (Matt. 2:23). There is a kind of play on words here; the Hebrew word for Nazareth is *Netzeret* and it is derived from the root, *netzer*, which means "branch". In effect then, Nazareth means something like "branch-town". Thus it is altogether fitting that the man whose name is "The Branch", who was a descendant of the royal line of David, should come from "branch-town", and should be known as "The Branch-man", or "the Nazarene". It is a bit difficult, of course, to appreciate a reference deeply rooted in a different language, but Zechariah's branch prophecy is actually a most elegant identification of the Messiah. Those familiar with Hebrew and the way its words are derived from definite roots would appreciate that the prophet was very accurate. In a similar case Micah identified Bethlehem, in Hebrew "Home of bread", as the birthplace of "the Bread of life". The Messiah's earthly life fascinatingly conforms to all that was said of Him in prophecy.

"Behold Your King"

With pinpoint accuracy Zechariah was able to predict the nature of the entrance of Messiah into the city of Jerusalem. Someone guessing at this event might have the King coming

in a most dramatic manner, perhaps even descending out
of heaven or at the head of a mighty army. Zechariah
foresaw with great clarity the career of Alexander the Great
in the first part of his ninth chapter. He was informed
about the ways of the mighty. But he prophesied most
humbly concerning the approach to Jerusalem of the King
of all:

> "Rejoice greatly, O daughter of Zion! Shout, O
> daughter of Jerusalem! Behold, your King is
> coming to you; He is just and having salvation,
> lowly and riding on a donkey, a colt, the foal of
> a donkey." (Zech. 9:9)

Where the fearsome Alexander was seen sweeping across
the nations on a great black horse, the Son of God would
enter the holy city on a donkey. The response of the people
of Jerusalem was to be one of rejoicing and welcome. And
indeed, as the Gospels relate, when the event actually came
to pass at the beginning of the Lord's last earthly week, He
bade His disciples to obtain a donkey. Two of His disciples
were to go into the nearby town of Bethphage, which was
on the crest of the Mt. of Olives, and there they would find a
donkey tied to a post with its colt. They were to tell the
owner that the Lord required it and they were to bring the
donkey to Jesus.

The Lord mounted the donkey on the summit of the Mt.
of Olives and rode the beast from there down into the
Kidron Valley and up to the Temple mount, through the
Eastern Gate. Those assembled on that initial Palm Sunday
did as Zechariah had admonished them to do. They cried
out *"Baruch hamelech haba bashem adonai,"* — "Blessed
is He who comes in the name of the Lord" (Matt. 21:11).
They waved palm branches and made the way of the
Lord into the city a triumphant procession. They
shouted, *"Hosanna,"* and they cried out all kinds of

Messianic titles and honors to the entering King.

The Pharisees were aghast, however. It appeared to them that they had lost their battle with a pretender to the Messianic throne and they finally exhorted Jesus Himself that the crowd reaction bordered on blasphemy. He should remonstrate with the people to refrain from saying those Messianic titles about Him, they said. But instead of rebuking His disciples, Jesus encouraged them, and He told the Pharisees that if the people stopped welcoming Him as King then the very stones on the ground would do it instead. God was determined that His Son would be welcomed into the city of the great King and that was all there was to that.

It should be appreciated that Jesus had a great following among the Jewish people of Israel at that time. It is too casually said that Israel missed the Messiah. They should have believed to the last man, but still a considerable number of Israelites had understood the prophecies or heard the teachings or seen the miracles or otherwise apprehended the fact that their King had come. Great throngs had attended Him from Galilee down to Jerusalem at the time of that Passover. Just previously they had seen the Lord raise His friend Lazarus from the dead. They were willing and eager to welcome Jesus as the promised Messiah. Even some of the leadership had believed in Him and were ready to accept Him as king.

But the majority had their way. It was only a matter of time before they would work their will to silence Him, they thought, forever. In any age, even today's, the remnant is still just a remnant and the majority do not realize the existence of God. One problem is, of course, the lack of knowledge of Messianic prophecy. We are stunned to see in the text that even Jesus' disciples did not understand the scene on the Mt. of Olives that day. Only after the resurrection were they cognizant that all of the Lord's actions answered to Zechariah's wonderful prediction:

His disciples did not understand these things at
first; but when Jesus was glorified, then they
remembered that these things were written
about Him and that they had done these things
to Him. (John 12:16)

Zechariah, like Daniel, understood the exploits of the
mighty and wrote of Alexander the Great. Both prophets in
their heavenly wisdom knew all about earthly kings, but
their pronouncements had to do with the King of Kings.

The Second Coming

Zechariah's description of the return of Messiah in His
second coming is clear and detailed, and it contrasts quite
a bit with the processional on the lowly donkey. This time,
the prophet tells us, Jesus will descend with power and
great glory from heaven itself. Once more He will approach
Jerusalem from the Mt. of Olives but with all of the
assembled hosts of heaven and all the power of the
universe. He will return to earth then at the place and "in
like manner" as He left in His ascension, just as the angels
predicted (Acts 1:11). The purpose of His return to the
earth will be, among other things, to conclude the War of
Armageddon at the end of the Tribulation. The Antichrist
will have gathered the armed forces of all nations on the
earth against Israel, Jerusalem, and the Lord. He will have
captured much of Jerusalem and will almost succeed in
destroying Israel and thus wiping the name of God off the
face of the earth forever. But when the Messiah returns,
remarkable things will occur on the Mt. of Olives over-
looking the city of God:

Behold, the day of the Lord is coming, and
your spoil will be divided in your midst.

> For I will gather all the nations to battle
> against Jerusalem; the city shall be taken, the
> houses rifled, and the women ravished. Half of
> the city shall go into captivity, but the
> remnant of people shall not be cut off from the
> city.
>
> Then the Lord will go forth and fight against
> those nations, as He fights in the day of battle.
>
> And in that day His feet will stand on the
> Mount of Olives, which faces Jerusalem on the
> east. And the Mount of Olives shall be split in
> two, from east to west, making a very large
> valley; half of the mountain shall move toward
> the north and half of it toward the south.
> (Zech. 14:1-4)

If the Antichrist thought he had the population of
Jerusalem trapped within those mountains that surround
the city, then the Lord will create a way out. The Mount of
Olives will split in half and create a large east-west valley
out of the city and the people will escape. They will go to a
community on the east side of the Mount of Olives called
Azle. After this rescue the Lord will go about to defeat the
Antichrist and his vast array of armies, with the saints of all
ages accompanying Him in this great and righteous task.

The Messiah will not only save Israel militarily but also
spiritually. We have quoted in several connections Zechariah's magnificent rendition of the reunion between
brethren.

> "And I will pour on the house of David and on
> the inhabitants of Jerusalem the Spirit of grace
> and supplication; they will look on Me whom
> they have pierced; they will mourn for Him as
> one mourns for his only son, and grieve for
> Him as one grieves for a firstborn. (Zech. 12:10)

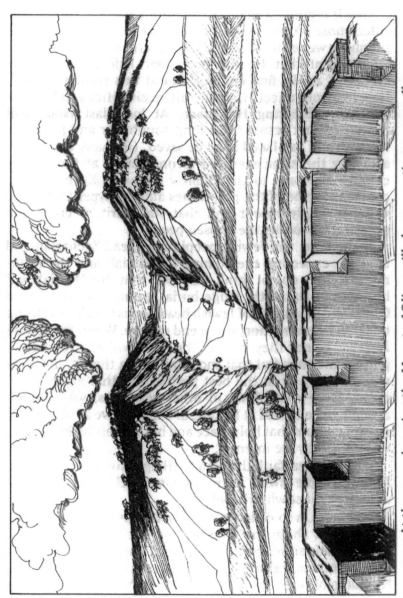

At the second coming the Mount of Olives will cleave, creating a new valley.

One is reminded again of the throne room of Joseph, the ruler whose brothers finally bow before him. In this singular prophecy we see that when Christ returns to the earth it will be apparent that He has been here before, for He was "pierced" at His first coming. But at this second coming, Israel will not reject Him but will receive Him and lead the world in accepting His grace. At long last Israel will recognize that Jesus is the long sought for and promised Messiah and "all Israel shall be saved" (Romans 11:26). We also saw the same scene of reconciliation at the second coming of Moses to the Hebrew slaves in Egypt. It is a constant theme of the prophecies and the types that Israel will ultimately repent and that the spirit of grace and supplication awaits the chosen people.

To be sure, the Jewish people have read Zechariah and they are expecting the coming of Messiah and the resurrection. They do not think, however, that this Messiah will be Jesus of Nazareth. Huge burial grounds on the Mt. of Olives and thousands of Jewish headstones testify to a strong belief in a resurrection at the end of time. When the Jewish Messiah comes they believe the dead will rise from their graves, and they feel that those buried on the Mt. of Olives will certainly be in the best position for that magnificent event. Even some Jews in other countries, who cannot arrange to be buried at the Mt. of Olives, have a little bag of soil taken from that holy place and buried beside their heads wherever they are interred.

With very real faith then, and perhaps a touch of irony, the Jewish people await their promised deliverer, primarily unaware of just who He will be.

Zechariah, a so-called minor prophet, provides invaluable information about the Messiah from the smallest detail to the most important celebrated events. His range is absolutely tremendous, extending from his own time well into the Kingdom of God, when he pictures the Messiah of Israel on

His throne in Jerusalem and the whole world coming up to
worship Him:

> And it shall come to pass that everyone who is
> left of all the nations which came against
> Jerusalem shall go up from year to year to
> worship the King, the Lord of hosts, and to keep
> the Feast of Tabernacles. (Zech. 14:16)

Obediently portraying his little dramas and patiently
writing the word of the Lord in most difficult times,
Zechariah predicted the betrayal of our Lord, the scattering
of the sheep, the name of the Messiah as the Branch, the
triumphal entry of the King into Jerusalem, the second
coming at the Mt. of Olives, the destruction of the armies of
the Antichrist, the salvation of Israel, and the establishment
of the kingdom of God upon the earth.

A current list of Zola Levitt's books, cassettes, albums, and videotapes is available at no charge from:

ZOLA
P.O. Box 12268
Dallas, Texas 75225